THE DAVINCI DECEPTION

Experience

LEADER'S WORKBOOK

DR. ERWIN W. LUTZER

Tyndale House Publishers, Carol Stream, Illinois

Visit Tyndale's exciting Web site at www.tyndale.com.

TYNDALE is a registered trademark of Tyndale House Publishers, Inc.
Tyndale's quill logo is a registered trademark of Tyndale House Publishers, Inc.

The Da Vinci Deception Experience Leader's Workbook

Contributing writer: Nate Conrad

Produced with the assistance of The Livingstone Corporation (www.livingstonecorp.com). Project staff includes David Veerman, Linda DeVries, Don Jones, Joel Bartlett, and Rachel Hawkins.

ISBN-13: 978-1-4143-1178-4
ISBN-10: 1-4143-1178-8

Printed in the United States of America

09 08 07 06 XXX 7 6 5 4 3 2 1

CONTENTS

Introduction to the Leader's Workbook v

SESSION ONE: Author's Note/Preface 1

SESSION TWO: Christianity, a Politician, and a Creed 13

SESSION THREE: That Other Bible 25

SESSION FOUR: Jesus, Mary Magdalene, and the Search for the Holy Grail . . 37

SESSION FIVE: Banned from the Bible: Why? 47

SESSION SIX: A Successful Search for Jesus 57

SESSION SEVEN: Divergent Paths: The Church and Its Competitors 67

Glossary 77

Reproducible Sheets 81

INTRODUCTION TO THE
LEADER'S WORKBOOK

The sections in this workbook guide will take the leader approximately 45 minutes to cover. Several optional materials are also included should the leader want to extend the time of the session to engage more with the book, DVD, and other secondary material like group activities, articles, reviews, and small group studies. Each lesson will include the following sections. These sections will help the leader design the session time and will include extra materials that may be needed to flesh out details, answer questions, or help participants apply what they are learning.

Lesson Introduction

The Introduction will give the leader a quick overview of where the lesson is headed and what should be accomplished or addressed in that specific session (Lesson Text). Participants should gain an understanding of the group's focus, the main idea, and the specific goals or objectives (Lesson Key Focus/Lesson Goals). The Lesson Materials are for the leader to assemble in preparation for the lesson and will incorporate a materials list for the main lesson content and the optional lesson content.

Lesson Format

Each lesson will follow the format laid out here. (Optional materials are included at the end.)

A. Welcome	3–5 minutes (2 facing pages)
B. Opening Activity (optional)	10 minutes
C. Intro to DVD	2 minutes
D. DVD segment	6 minutes, except first video (17 minutes)
E. DVD Segment Recap	10 minutes (optional)
F. Message	12–15 minutes (2 facing pages)
G. Biblical Study (optional)	20–30 minutes (2 facing pages)
H. Small Group Discussion	20–30 minutes (1 page)
I. Personal Application (optional)	5–7 minutes (1 page)
J. Homework	3–5 minutes
K. Handouts and Worksheets	2–3 minutes
a. Chapter Quiz	
b. Chapter Summary	
c. Personal Response	
L. Other Resources (optional)	No time frame

Welcome: 3–5 minutes

The purpose of this section is to welcome the participants to the session and to cover the previous week's material as well as the current session's objectives. This will help keep you on track, as well as other small group leaders who may be working with you.

Opening Activity (optional): 10–15 minutes

This section will give you one or two options for each session in order to engage the group, get them talking, and help them to get to know each other. These activities may require extra materials and preparation, as well as interaction among participants.

Intro to DVD: 2–3 minutes

Preview the DVD beforehand so you can give a brief synopsis. You may also want to prepare the audience with questions you want them to think about while they watch. Give this information to the audience before viewing the DVD segment together. The first video will require a little more preparation as you will need to share background on who Dr. Erwin Lutzer is and why we would want to hear from him.

DVD Segment: 6 minutes (except first video, 17 minutes)

Preview the DVD material so you are confident about what it contains, how it fits into the study for the evening, and what elements you may want to incorporate into the message or small group discussion times.

DVD Segment Recap (optional): 10 minutes

If you have time, or if you feel this is important for your particular group to grasp what is being discussed in the DVD segment, prepare some questions for following up the DVD. You may want to ask questions about implications, comprehension, or clarification.

Message: 12–15 minutes

Participants should leave with sound teaching and a clear objective from the session. Thus, you may want to include a brief time to incorporate the Dr. Lutzer teaching, the material in the book, and the connection to Scripture. Bringing the material together this way will allow you as the leader to integrate all that has been discussed in the session. You will be able to craft what participants will walk away with, including personal application, clarification, or further information that may be helpful for where your particular group is at spiritually, relationally, and doctrinally.

Biblical Study: 20–30 minutes

Since we are dealing with overt heresy that has been disseminated for centuries, it is important that you as the leader clarify the heresies and refute them with Scripture. The biblical studies are meant to bring participants back to the Word, to sit under its instruction, and to learn the truth of its claims about God's relentless love, the deity and work of Christ, salvation, and other tenets of the true Christian faith that are being called into question as a result of *The Da Vinci Code*.

Small Group Discussion: 20–30 minutes

In response to each DVD segment and the book material it covers, this guide encourages leaders to allow for members of the group to engage with the statements made by Brown and Dr. Lutzer. Politics and religion have a way of pressing emotional buttons. We respond with passion, joy, anger, and confusion when our convictions are called into question. We may respond with joy when others ask our opinion; we may be angry when what we have invested our lives into is being challenged. The small group discussion materials will not only allow members to respond with their feelings but also to respond as a group as they turn to the Bible for the answers to accusations made by *The Da Vinci Code*.

Allowing participants to share their questions, responses, and feelings will help the group take ownership of the material and help them invest. These matters are critical to the health of the church, now and fifty years from now.

The group discussion time is prefaced by a list of small group leader hints and helps. The small group leaders should be participants who can commit to attend each week and who are willing to come prepared for the session. Each small group leader should have the strength to allow for open discussion while keeping his or her group moving toward the lesson's goals and objectives.

Personal Application (optional): 5–7 minutes

This section is an optional time to be used in the session or elsewhere. It may include take-home ideas for participants to help them reflect on what has been addressed in the session or in the book. As in all study of Scripture, there is a call to respond. Thus, even in what is perceived to be an academic rebuttal to the claims of Brown's book, we need to make personal application, responding to the truths of the Gospel and how it counters our tendency to make God, the Word, and salvation into a works-oriented righteousness, instead of the gracious, merciful act that it truly is.

Homework (optional): 3–5 minutes

This section will include optional materials that you may hand out or allude to. As the leader, you may want to focus on a given part of Dr. Lutzer's book. Handing out a reading for participants to use between sessions will provide an opportunity to continue discussion with other participants or with peers, coworkers, and family members who have also read Brown's book. This material should complement what you are doing in the group session and should not be burdensome. Use these optional ideas for longer session times or for outside study.

Handouts and Worksheets: 2–3 minutes

At the end of every session, you should take time to talk through the "homework" assignment. The purpose of these assignments is to drive home the teaching that has gone on at the current session and give the participant the opportunity for further application and study of the material. Hand out the following sheets to all the participants:

1. Chapter Quiz (1 page)
2. Summary Sheet of the week's chapter of Dr. Lutzer's book (1 page)
3. Personal Response (1 page)

Other Resources (optional): No Time Frame

You may choose to use these supplementary materials in your message text or to incorporate them into additional handouts. You can also make these resources available to the group and have them do research and study of these articles, books, transcripts, etc. Some of these resources will come at an additional charge or will only be available to subscribers of magazines. Use your judgment in how you will use these optional materials. This section is not calculated in the overall time that it will take to run your session.

The Da Vinci Code book and movie are causing people of all faiths across America to ask historically significant questions. Because of such a widespread response, *The Da Vinci Deception Experience* provides a marvelous outreach opportunity for your congregation and community. It will serve as a resource for developing answers and correcting misperceptions. For maximum impact, be sure to publicize the event as much as possible through posters, bulletins, press releases, etc. And have plenty of *The Da Vinci Deception* books on hand for distribution. Paperback versions are now available at Christian bookstores.

SESSION ONE:
· AUTHOR'S NOTE / PREFACE

This session is a kick-off event for a six-session series. It is designed to engage attendees and encourage them to return for the remainder of the series. This preliminary event features an entertaining and captivating 17-minute multimedia presentation. The video will jump-start the series and fuel discussion. Beforehand, encourage your core group to ask questions in their respective communities to determine the common perceptions about *The Da Vinci Code*. During this kick-off session, be sure to have plenty of copies of *The Da Vinci Deception* on hand.

Introduction

LESSON TEXT
Dr. Lutzer, Author's Note and Preface

LESSON KEY FOCUS/IDEA
The purpose of this session is to present the material presented in Dan Brown's book *The Da Vinci Code* to the listening audience. Students will learn the various assertions set forth by Brown's book, including the discrepancies and errors as determined through scholarly research in the archeological, theological, and historical fields.

LESSON GOALS
1. To introduce the audience to the heresies in *The Da Vinci Code*
2. To respond to those heresies with Scripture
3. To engage the audience in such a way that they will return for the subsequent six sessions
4. To promote Dr. Lutzer's book for purchase, a required reading for the sessions

LESSON MATERIALS
The Da Vinci Deception books, Bibles, pens, paper, handouts, small group questions, DVD, small prizes for quiz results (such as small candy bars or hard candy)

Lesson Format

A. Welcome	5 minutes
B. Opening Activities (optional)	10 minutes
C. Intro to DVD	2–3 minutes
D. DVD Segment	17 minutes
E. DVD Segment Recap (optional)	10 minutes
F. Message	12–15 minutes
G. Biblical Study	0 minutes: no study for the first lesson
H. Small Group Discussion	30 minutes
I. Homework	5 minutes
J. Handouts and Worksheets	5 minutes

    a. Chapter Quiz

    b. Chapter Summary

    c. Gospels of John and Mark

    d. Personal Response

K. Personal Application/Response (optional)	15 minutes
L. Other Resources (optional)	

Notes from Christian Book Guides' Web site

As the leader, you may want to include these notes in your message or in introductory materials for the audience. The audience needs to understand the nature of the course and what it seeks to accomplish. They also need to understand the basic premise of the book. The following paragraphs adapted from **www. christianbookguides.com** will be helpful.

The controversial novel *The Da Vinci Code* rocketed up the fiction best seller charts and has remained at or near the top of the list for months. While the novel is a fictional work, many readers believe that it is based on a true conspiracy on the part of the church and those in power to manipulate Christianity to suit their own purposes. The book calls into question the authority of the Bible and the veracity of what Christians believe about Jesus Christ. Many readers, Christian and not, are not treating *The Da Vinci Code* as fictional entertainment but as an accurate portrayal of church history and are being misled by false doctrine. It is important for Christians to understand *The Da Vinci Code*, in order to respond to those who are taking the claims of the book seriously, are finding their faith shaken by it, or are mistaking it as a reliable source of historical fact.

Tentatively scheduled as a major motion picture release in summer 2006, and directed by Ron Howard, *The Da Vinci Code* will continue to be a hotbed of intense interest and discussion. *The Da Vinci Deception* illuminates the historical truth readers need to know, to give intelligent responses to the malicious attacks on Christianity as found in *The Da Vinci Code*.

A. Welcome: 5 minutes

1. Welcome participants to the session. Thank everyone for coming, and tell them where the books can be purchased, where they can pick up coffee or snacks, and the timing of the break if you choose to have one.

2. Explain the purpose of this class—why you are covering *The Da Vinci Deception* (from Author's Note, p. xiv):

    a. To investigate the historical roots of Christianity

    b. To give credible answers to questions such as:

        i. Who is Jesus?

        ii. Is the New Testament a reliable source?

        iii. What should this mean to us in the twenty-first century?

3. Review the goals for the current session:

    a. To introduce the heresies in *The Da Vinci Code*

    b. To motivate everyone to return for the subsequent six sessions

    c. To promote Dr. Lutzer's book for purchase, a required reading for the sessions

4. Quickly review the book *The Da Vinci Code* with the audience:

    a. Author: Dan Brown

    b. Published: 2004

    c. Books sold to date: *The Da Vinci Code* has sold over 25 million books in 44 languages.

    d. The nature of the book.

5. Ask preliminary questions of the audience about the book before watching the video and starting the session:

    a. Who here has read *The Da Vinci Code*?

    b. What do you think are the points of contention in the book?

    c. What issues raised in the book concern you? Why?

    d. What questions do you hope to have answered in these sessions?

    e. Why are you here? What are you hoping to glean from these sessions?

6. Open in a word of prayer to begin the session, praying for:

    a. Clarity—to understand the nature and nuances of the book

    b. Courage—to talk about issues with friends, families, colleagues

    c. Wisdom—to discern truth in articles, books, reviews, etc. that will be considered

B. Opening Activities (optional): 10 minutes

TO TELL THE TRUTH

Divide into groups of three to five. Have members face each other and briefly introduce themselves. Explain that the purpose is to have a little fun and get to know each other more. Then explain that each person is to make three statements about himself or herself—two of these statements should be true, and one should not be true. After each person has shared, the group should try to determine which of the three statements is false.

For example, I may share:

1. I have never met my biological parents.
2. I once had three front teeth.
3. I have been off the continent.

(*The lie for me is statement 3—I have never been off the continent.*)

Use yourself as an example to give people an idea for what they might share. Then have the groups begin. (Note: This may take some time as people find this deception very humorous, and conversations will lead to the stories behind the true statements.)

I NEVER

This is another get-to-know-you game. In small groups of five to ten, have everyone gather in a circle and hold up ten fingers. Then, one at a time, going around the circle, each person states something that he or she has *never done* that the person believes that most everyone else in the group has done. Then whoever *has* done that activity puts down a finger. A person might say, for example, "I have never traveled outside the United States." Then, everyone in the group who has traveled outside the USA would have to put down a finger. When a person has lowered all ten fingers, he or she is eliminated. The person with any finger(s) still "standing" wins.

C. Introduction to DVD and Erwin Lutzer: 2–3 minutes

After the activity or the prayer, take a few minutes to preface the DVD and to introduce Dr. Erwin Lutzer as a good background.

1. Who is Erwin Lutzer and why should we listen to him?
   a. Dr. Erwin W. Lutzer, senior pastor of The Moody Church since 1980, was born and reared near Regina, Saskatchewan, Canada. Dr. Lutzer is an award-winning author of more than twenty books, a celebrated international conference speaker, and the featured speaker on three radio programs: *The Moody Church Hour, Songs in the Night*, and *Running to Win*. These programs are available on the Moody Broadcasting Network, the Bible Broadcasting Network, Trans World Radio, and many Christian radio stations around the world. Dr. Lutzer and his wife, Rebecca, live in the Chicago area and are the parents of three married children.
   b. Dan Brown's best-selling novel *The Da Vinci Code*, blurs the lines between history and fiction, leaving readers wondering, "Could this really be true?" By distorting the truth, Brown implies that Christianity is based on a lie. In his book *The Da Vinci Deception*, Dr. Lutzer examines the alleged "facts" behind the fiction and provides clear and authoritative answers to the confusion surrounding the life of Jesus and the Christian faith. Whether or not you have read Brown's novel, you will gain a new understanding of the issues presented and the historical basis of early Christianity.

2. What should I watch for on the DVD?(Fill in questions here from your personal previewing of the DVD:)

    a.

    b.

    c.

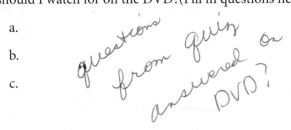 *questions from quiz answered on DVD?*

D. DVD Segment: 17 minutes

As a leader, preview the DVD and prepare the group with questions to think about as they watch the segment. Share with the audience what the DVD segment will cover and how it will coincide with the book by Dr. Lutzer.

E. DVD Segment Recap (optional): 10 minutes

Ask questions to recap the DVD and to call attention to items that are important and that will be addressed in the message and in small groups. You could ask, for example:

1. What issues did the video raise that concern you?
2. What statements in the video segment were you not aware of?
3. How have you been exposed already to the material presented in *The Da Vinci Code*?
4. How do you think these sessions will help you connect to others who have read the book?

If desired, you can do this in small groups and expand the number and breadth of questions asked.

F. Message: 10–12 minutes

Say something like the following:

In the author's note at the beginning of his book, Dr. Lutzer quotes Justin Pope in an article from the *Chicago Sun-Times*, February 13, 2004, p. 48: "There's black Jesus, and white Jesus. Homely and handsome, capitalist and socialist, stern and hippie. Hardworking social reformer, mystical comforter."

Throughout *The Da Vinci Code*, Brown has called into question, in the same way that many have before him, the character named Jesus as described in the New Testament Scriptures. Along with hundreds of other writers and philosophers throughout history, Brown has created a Jesus based on his liking, based on what makes him most comfortable and least likely to squirm.

The idea that a man would claim to be God and make demands of people regarding service, sacrifice, love, and forgiveness is a hard pill to swallow. Come up with some good ideas, yes, that is fine . . . talk about how the world should be, that is okay too, but to claim to be the only way of salvation, to have the only right answer, to call people sinners, unholy in the sight of God and justly deserving punishment . . . well, then you have gone too far.

In the novel *The Da Vinci Code*, Brown reveals several "truths" that, supposedly, have been suppressed for hundreds of years:

- Jesus married Mary Magdalene.
- They had children who intermarried with the French royal line.
- The Catholic Church is made up of greedy, power-hungry, male chauvinists trying to subdue women.
- A secret organization in the Catholic Church is trying to keep the world from knowing the truth.

Regarding these "truths," Brown claims to have done extensive research and says many of the claims stated in the book, a fictional novel, are in fact, true and being kept quiet. So we have a blending of truth and lore, fiction and fact. We have a genre, a type of literature, that is being passed off as true theological, archeological research. Readers on both sides of *The Da Vinci Code* need to accurately understand what is being stated and the danger of reading a novel that claims to be true.

In the book *The Da Vinci Deception* and the video segments we'll be watching, Dr. Lutzer will clarify the truth claims that Brown has made in his book, debunking the falsified evidence, and address and steer readers to the truth of Scripture. It is important for us as students of the Word to be immersed in God's Word in order to be able to refute false accusations or heretical teachings when they come. And they will. For hundreds of years, men and women have taught doctrine and theology that does not coincide with the teaching of the Old and New Testament Scriptures. And yet, Scripture remains, and God continues to move and work in the world, changing men and women, redeeming them and reconciling them to himself.

Brown reports the following:

1. The Gnostic Gospels are a more accurate presentation of Jesus and the early church.
2. Jesus was not God at all, and Constantine invented the deity of Christ.
3. Jesus and Mary were married and had a little girl.
4. The early church knew that sex rituals connected them to the divine, and the Catholic Church did not like this, so they made sex out to be a disgusting and sinful act.
5. The Catholic Church is covering all this up to keep women subdued.
6. Jesus was killed on the cross and did not rise again; rather, Mary and her daughter went to Gaul and intermarried with the French.
7. Jesus wanted Mary to found the church, not Peter—that is why he told everyone that she was a prostitute.
8. Leonardo da Vinci knew all this and was hiding details in artwork, sculptures, and more.

Scripture says, among other things, that:

1. Mark 2:5–12—Jesus has the power to forgive sins.
2. Mark 14:61–62—Jesus claimed to be the Son of God.
3. John 1:1–14—Jesus is both God and man.
4. John 14:6—Jesus is the only way to the Father.

[handwritten notes: "new age", "yesterday Kabbalah Scientology", "scriptures about false doctrine today Da Vinci code tomorrow?"]

5. 1 Peter 2:22–24—Jesus never sinned; he died on the cross, and his wounds have healed us.

6. 1 John 1:1–3—An eyewitness describes the Savior.

One reviewer of *The Da Vinci Code*, Jana Krause on Amazon.com said this:

> Is what *The Da Vinci Code* proposes true? Well, the research is correct. The historical events and people explored in the book are real. But no one knows the Truth. . . . nor will we ever, probably. I think that some things are meant to be a mystery. With all the world's diverse religions and each individual's belief in what is Divine—the Truth would have to destroy the beliefs, hopes, and lives of many of the world's population. So, perhaps, in the divine scheme of things, there are many more Truths than one. Don't take the book too seriously. Just read it and enjoy!

If Scripture is true, the Truth, as Krause said, would destroy the beliefs, hopes and lives of many of the world's population. How can we know? How can we be sure? What of all the other world's religions? What happens to them if the gospel as it is relayed in the Bible is true?

If what Dan Brown purports to be true is in fact true, and the gospel recorded in the New Testament is blatantly false and the result of a Catholic Church conspiracy at the Council of Nicaea, then what does that imply for Christians everywhere? What does this mean for Catholics, Lutherans, Presbyterians, Methodists, Baptists, and other denominations that herald Jesus Christ as Lord and Savior, the Redeemer of men and women?

That is why we are here. That is what we will explore over the next six weeks as we read from Dr. Lutzer, hear him speak, and study the Word of God. It is no wonder that *The Da Vinci Code* has caused such a scare for some. Doubt has been cast on the veracity of Scripture, and those who have written and compiled it in the canon as we know it. You may know others who are struggling, or who have, or when the movie comes out may be shaken by the possibility of this "code" being true. In the next several weeks, we'll take a look at that which Brown has called into question. We will together explore the truths and lies that have been floating about *The Da Vinci Code*.

The purpose of the sessions and the book that Dr. Lutzer wrote is not to address all the inaccuracies or poor research, but 1) to understand where breakdowns occur, and 2) to address some particular questions that will help us respond to attacks against Christianity, including the following questions delineated in the Preface, pp. xxviii-xxix:

1. Did Constantine invent the deity of Christ?
2. Are the Gnostic Gospels reliable guides to early church history?
3. Who determined what New Testament books would be included?
4. Is it plausible that Mary Magdalene and Jesus were married?
5. Was Opus Dei charged with suppressing the real story of Jesus?
6. Is it true that Gnosticism is a viable form of Christianity?
7. If we agree on God, do we have to agree on Jesus too?

G. Biblical Study (optional)

This section is designed for a biblical study of related passages in small groups. There is no biblical study for the first session.

H. Small Group Discussion (optional): 30 minutes

If you have time or want to expand your time with the group, have small group leaders work through the handout on page 83 in small groups as a wrap-up to your time together. Close the session in the large group and go over the homework and optional personal application materials with them.

1. *The DaVinci Code* is a work of fiction. Why are people taking its claims so seriously? (Answer: *The author asks readers to take its claims seriously. Also, the author has indicated that he truly believes the conspiracy theory about which he is writing.*)

2. What is the harm in a fiction book like *The DaVinci Code*? (Answer: *Because the author claims that his story is based in fact, gullible people could be deceived. Knowledgeable people won't be sucked in by the heresies, but most readers don't have the grounding in church history and theology to be able to discern fact from fiction.*)

3. What do you think was the agenda that the author, Dan Brown, had in writing this novel? (Answer: *His agenda was to attack orthodox Christianity and the truth of the Gospels and to promote a feminist and Gnostic view of Jesus.*)

4. What might be some clues that the author has crossed the line between a purely fictional story and a propaganda piece? (Answer: *He claims that the story is based on truth.*)

5. How likely is it that orthodox Christian theology is merely a sinister hoax perpetrated on innocent people? (Answer: *It's not likely, given that it has stood the test of time, while conspiracy theories like the Da Vinci Code have come and gone over the centuries.*)

6. Why do you think some people are attracted to conspiracy theories? (Answer: *Some possibilities: They are intriguing; people love a mystery; and such theories are unprovable since the evidence is being hidden by the conspirators.*)

I. Homework: 5–7 minutes

1. Purchase the Dr. Lutzer book so you can follow along with the rest of the group.

2. Read the preface, "*The Da Vinci Code* at a Glance," and Chapter One, "Christianity, a Politician, and a Creed."

    a. Underline and mark up the book as you read.

    b. Write down any questions you have as you come across the material.

    c. Read through the text with your Bible at the ready, and look up verses and read Scripture in response and addition to what is in the *Dr. Lutzer* book.

3. Read the Gospel of John and the Gospel of Mark to get an overview of the Jesus as described in the New Testament.

4. Listen to Dan Brown's lecture at New Hampshire Writers' Project, available on Dan Brown's Web site.

5. In his lecture at the New Hampshire Writers' Project, Brown makes this statement:

"Interestingly, if you ask three people what it means to be Christian, you will get three different answers. Some feel being baptized is sufficient. Others feel you must accept the Bible as absolute historical fact. Still others require a belief that all those who do not accept Christ as their personal Savior are doomed to hell. Faith is a continuum, and we each fall on that line where we may. By attempting to rigidly classify ethereal concepts like faith, we end up debating semantics to the point where we entirely miss the obvious—that is, that we are all trying to decipher life's big mysteries, and we're each following our own paths of enlightenment. I consider myself a student of many religions. The more I learn, the more questions I have. For me, the spiritual quest will be a lifelong work in progress."

    a. How do you respond to this?

    b. What concerns you? What seems right about what he has said?

    c. What are the implications to this?

    d. If you were asked to give a rebuttal using Scripture, what would you include?

J. Handouts and Worksheets: 5 minutes

Have several copies of the handouts to give to your group members this week.

difference between Gnostic & agnostic

CHAPTER QUIZ (p. 83)

1. What claims are made in Dan Brown's book *The Da Vinci Code*? p. xvii —
2. With what family line has Brown proposed that Jesus is connected? p. xx
3. What purpose does Opus Dei play in the book? p. xxii
4. What was the responsibility of the Knights Templar? Who were supposed members? p. xx
5. According to Brown and his research, who should have succeeded Jesus in leading Christianity? p. xxi
6. Why did this not happen? p. xxi
7. What is the Shekinah? p. xxiv
8. According to one of the characters in the book, the New Testament is the result of what? p. xxiv-xxv

Holy Grail — *mithras Gnostic Bible briefly*

CHAPTER SUMMARY (p. 84)

The Da Vinci Code proposes the following truths that readers may never have heard because of the supposed Catholic Church's suppression of these shattering truths:

1. Jesus and Mary Magdalene were married.
2. They had a daughter, Sarah, who married into the French royalty, the Merovingians.
3. This daughter may have had children and this lineage of Christ may still be alive even today.

In addition, the Catholic Church has been killing people to keep these and other secrets safe. An organization, Opus Dei, has been charged with protecting the truth about the life of Christ and Mary. Ancient codes and hidden truths have been implanted into paintings, music, and sculpture for centuries by the Priory of Sion and its military branch, the Knights Templar, which included members such as Victor Hugo, Isaac Newton, Mozart, and Leonardo da Vinci.

Jesus had intended for Mary Magdalene to continue the leadership of the church after he was crucified. Peter and other men did not like this, so they portrayed her as a prostitute to defame her and keep her from leadership. So the church is really the establishment of male chauvinists who are power hungry.

The "truth" is found in Old Testament verses that tell us there is a female counterpart to the male representation of God, called the Shekinah. The church hated this goddess worship and enabling of women and so doctored the Scriptures to eliminate this aspect and hence oppress women. In order to be fully enlightened as a Christian, these sources say, one must engage in sexual rituals which allow men and women to truly experience God. Of course the church hated sex, so they made it out to be a "disgusting and sinful act."

Brown goes on to claim that these secrets can be known to anyone, they are not really secrets. His research netted academia's finest who were ready and willing to talk about the truth of Christ as known in the Gnostic Gospels.

Dr. Lutzer finishes the introductory material with a call to research of his own, to study the veracity of the Scripture and to find the truth, dispelling lore and fabrications, and call readers to a right view of the Jesus as found in the New Testament.

THE GOSPELS OF JOHN AND MARK (p. 85)

Read the Gospel of Mark and/or the Gospel of John before the next session to get to know the Jesus of the New Testament. If you have read enough about the Jesus as known to the Gnostics, or Brown's Jesus, compare that with what you are reading in the Gospel of Mark or John.

1. What sorts of acts did Jesus perform as recorded in the New Testament?
2. How did Jesus interact with the women who were around him in ministry?
3. What is your perception of his view of women?
4. What was Jesus' view of himself?
5. What view of Jesus did the disciples have?
6. What claims did Jesus make in the text you are reading?
7. What questions are raised for you that you could ask someone who knows Scripture well?

PERSONAL RESPONSE (p. 86)
Review the material in the Personal Response section and provide copies for the participants.

K. Personal/Application Response (optional): 15 minutes

In your personal study or quiet time, think through the following questions:

1. Consider the quote from Dr. Lutzer's book, "There's black Jesus, and white Jesus. Homely and handsome, capitalist and socialist, stern and hippie. Hardworking social reformer, mystical comforter" (Justin Pope).
    a. How have I created Jesus in my own eyes?
    b. How have I restricted Jesus to be what I want?
2. Does *The Da Vinci Code* cause me to doubt?
    a. How? Why?
    b. How do I respond to this doubt?
3. Looking honestly at my personal study, am I familiar enough with Scripture to interact well with a book like *The Da Vinci Code*? Where am I strong? Where am I lacking?

L. Other Resources (optional)

Consider the following resources this week if you have time:

1. Articles to consider:
    a. Dan Brown's interview on his Web site (it is paraphrased).
    b. Articles refuting the claims of *The Da Vinci Code*.
    c. Articles supporting the claims of *The Da Vinci Code*.

2. Books to consider:
    a. Lutzer, Erwin, *The Da Vinci Deception*
    b. Olson and Miesel, *The Da Vinci Hoax*

3. Video/TV/Internet:
    a. View the Sony Web site for the movie, and check out the trailer.
    b. View *The Da Vinci Code* Web site.
    c. Watch *National Treasure*, the PG-rated, Nicholas Cage movie. It is similar in "symbology" as the treasure is hidden mystically in the Declaration of Independence, dollar bills, and more.
    d. Play an audio segment for the group from Dan Brown at the New Hampshire Writers' Project, minute 14:42 to 18:45.

SESSION TWO:
CHRISTIANITY, A POLITICIAN, AND A CREED

Introduction

LESSON TEXT

Dr. Lutzer, Chapter One: "Christianity, a Politician, and a Creed"

LESSON KEY FOCUS/IDEA

The purpose of this session is:

1. To debunk the proposition that the Council of Nicaea, called by Constantine, was an attempt by the early church to fabricate a list of texts that support male exclusivity and to "create" the deity of Jesus.
2. To communicate the truth of what happened at the Council of Nicaea.

LESSON GOALS

As a result of this session, participants will:

1. Know the truth about Constantine and the nature of the Council of Nicaea.
2. Learn the deity of Christ was understood and believed by the early church long before the council of Nicaea.
3 Discover that the material presented by Dan Brown has circulated for years as a heresy of the true Christian gospel.

LESSON MATERIALS

The Da Vinci Deception books, Bibles, pens, paper, handouts, small group questions, DVD

LESSON FORMAT

A. Welcome	3–5 minutes
B. Opening Activities (optional)	10–15 minutes
C. Intro to DVD	2 minutes
D. DVD Segment	6 minutes
E. Small Group Discussion	30 minutes
F. Biblical Study (optional)	30 minutes
G. Message	10–12 minutes
H. Homework	5 minutes in session

I. Handouts and Worksheets   5 minutes
    a. Chapter Quiz
    b. Chapter Summary
    c. Personal Response
J. Other Resources (optional)

A. Welcome: 3–5 minutes

1. Welcome everyone back, and greet new people who may have joined the group.
2. Explain to participants why you are covering *The Da Vinci Deception* (from Author's Note, p. xiii):
    a. Investigate the historical roots of Christianity
    b. Give credible answers to questions like these:
        i. Who is Jesus?
        ii. Is the New Testament a reliable source?
        iii. What should this mean to us in the twenty-first century?
3. Review last week's material (preface) with the group: what was covered and what the group should have done to prepare for the present session.
4. Give overview of what the group will do at the current session:
    a. Learn the truth about Constantine and the nature of the Council of Nicaea.
    b. Understand that the deity of Christ was firmly established and believed by the early church well before the Council of Nicaea.
    c. Know that the material presented by Dan Brown is heresy that has circulated for many years and has been refuted already.

B. Opening Activities (optional): 10–15 minutes

"EMPEROR CONSTANTINE THE GREAT"

Have individuals work alone or in teams of three to come up with as many words as they can, using only the letters in the name "Emperor Constantine the Great." For example: map, tea, roar, constant, greet, terror, etc. After five minutes, have the group with the longest list of words come up and read their list. Have two or three teams read, with other members crossing off identical words. Tally the totals and give a prize to the top two teams.

QUIZ

Give this quiz on historical elements of Christianity (related or unrelated to the DVD) as an icebreaker and an illustration of how we often read things with a lot of trust assuming that the source we are reading is reliable. This can be given orally or on paper.

1. In what year was the Council of Nicaea convened? (Answer: *AD 325*)
2. In what year did Luther nail to the church door the 95 Theses? (Answer: *1517*)
3. What was the name of the church? (Answer: *Wittenberg Cathedral*)
4. What English monarch caused the church in England to break with the church in Rome? (Answer: *Henry VIII*)
5. Which Pope stopped the barbarian invasion of Rome? (Answer: *Gregory of Nyssa*)
6. Who was the founder of the modern missionary movement? (Answer: *Hudson Taylor*)
7. Who was the only disciple to die a natural death? (Answer: *John*)
8. "God helps those who help themselves" is in Scripture—true or false? (Answer: *False—Benjamin Franklin said it*)
9. Who is believed to be buried beneath St. Peter's Cathedral in Rome? (Answer: *St. Peter*)

C. Intro to DVD: 2 minutes

Beforehand, preview the DVD and prepare the group with questions to think about as they watch the segment. Share with the participants what the DVD segment will cover and how it will coincide with the book by Dr. Lutzer.

D. DVD Segment: 6 minutes

Watch the DVD segment together. Afterward, divide into small groups to work through the small group material: pages 15–18.

Questions that as a leader you want to have the participants address:

1.

2.

3.

E. Small Group Discussion: 30 minutes

SMALL GROUP LEADER NOTES

After the DVD, break into small groups. All small group leaders should have copies of handouts for the session. The purpose of the small group discussions is to help participants of the group interact with the material on a personal level, to encourage participants to share their experiences, and their responses, and to study together.

SMALL GROUP LEADER HELPS

1. Small groups should be safe places to discuss and interact with the material. So . . .
    a. Don't monopolize the conversations or allow a group member to do so.
    b. Ask open-ended questions:
        i. How might someone respond to what Dr. Lutzer said?
        ii. How might you interact with others who have read the book?
        iii. What concerns do you have based on what you have read or seen?
        iv. What Bible verses relate directly to what we are reading and hearing?
2. Prepare in advance so you have additional material or questions.
3. Incorporate material from both the book and the video segments.
4. Small groups should be a place to discuss the Bible together.
5. Small groups should be where God works in people's lives, so be sure to take a moment at the end to pray for how you can use the material to interact with peers, friends, and family.

PRELIMINARY SMALL GROUP DISCUSSION QUESTIONS

1. Before Constantine's conversion to Christianity, what was life in Rome like for Christians? (Answer: *They were persecuted for not worshipping Caesar as well as Christ.*)
2. Constantine is credited with making Rome safe for Christians as a result of converting to Christianity himself. What were the circumstances of his conversion? (Answer: *On the eve of battle, Constantine saw a vision of Christ. The battle was successful, and Constantine became ruler of the empire. He issued the Edict of Milan to halt the persecution of Christians.*)
3. Why did Constantine convene the Council of Nicaea? (Answer: *He wanted to resolve doctrinal disputes.*)
4. What effects were various doctrinal disputes having on Constantinople in Constantine's day? (Answer: *They were divisive and threatening the unity of the empire.*)
5. What heresies did the Council of Nicaea address? (Answer: *The Council considered—and rejected— claims that Jesus was not divine and that he was not one with God.*)
6. What arguments were made against these theories? (Answer: *If Christ is not God, then he could not redeem mankind. Also, he created all things and therefore could not have been created himself by someone else.*)
7. Why is it unlikely that Christ's divinity was "invented" at the Council of Nicaea? (Answer: *It was claimed by Jesus himself, by the apostles, and by early church leaders centuries before the council took place.*)
8. How did the biblical canon come to be chosen? Was it a function of the Council of Nicaea? (Answer: *The canon was chosen through careful study and consensus that books met certain criteria and were the result of God's revelation. The process was not a function of the Council of Nicaea.*)
9. What philosophies were the church leaders supposedly promoting, according to *The Da Vinci Code*? (Answer: *They allegedly advocated male dominance and the suppression of women.*)
10. Erwin Lutzer states that the Romans were "tolerant of everyone except those who were intolerant" (see p. 22). Do you find this attitude to be in evidence today? How so? (Answer: *Political correctness, thinking that all paths lead to God, widespread acceptance of immorality, intolerance toward Christians, etc., are examples.*)

FURTHER SMALL GROUP DISCUSSION QUESTIONS (SELECT A FEW QUESTIONS IN ADVANCE OF THE SESSION)

1. On page 5, under "Welcome to the Council," Dr. Lutzer writes about the nature of the early church and their passion for scriptural integrity and a sound understanding of what was being promulgated in churches and smaller circles.
   a. What do you think of the passion that people had for doctrinal integrity?
   b. How is the twenty-first century perspective different? Give support for your response.
   c. What do you think has contributed to the change?
   d. Where are you along the continuum of "doctrinal passion"?
   e. Why is this question important? What implications does it have for the reader in the twenty-first century?

2. You have heard people talk about the nature of the Trinity in several different ways.
   a. What are the best illustrations you have heard (e.g., the egg has three parts; three fingers touching the table; three intertwined rings of gold)?
   b. How are these helpful to Christianity?
   c. In what ways are they problematic?

3. What do you think of Marcellus' response on page 7?

4. How often do you use creeds in your worship services? Which creeds does your church use?
   a. What are the benefits of the creeds? How are they helpful?
   b. What is the danger of a creed? How can it be harmful?

5. Without reviewing the book, what are the implications for changing the word *similar* to *same* in the Nicene Creed (see creed below)?

6. After discussion, go back and read over pages 8–9 to consider the implications of the change in one word. What might this mean for us today?

The Nicene Creed

I believe in one God, the Father Almighty, Maker of heaven and earth, and of all things visible and invisible.

And in one Lord Jesus Christ, the only-begotten Son of God, begotten of the Father before all worlds; God of God, Light of Light, very God of very God; begotten, not made, being of one substance with the Father, by whom all things were made.

Who, for us men for our salvation, came down from heaven, and was incarnate by the Holy Spirit of the virgin Mary, and was made man; and was crucified also for us under Pontius Pilate; He suffered and was buried; and the third day He rose again, according to the Scriptures; and ascended into heaven, and sits on the right hand of the Father; and He shall come again, with glory, to judge the quick and the dead; whose kingdom shall have no end.

And I believe in the Holy Ghost, the Lord and Giver of Life; who proceeds from the Father and the Son; who with the Father and the Son together is worshipped and glorified; who spoke by the prophets.

And I believe one holy catholic and apostolic Church. I acknowledge one baptism for the remission of sins; and I look for the resurrection of the dead, and the life of the world to come. Amen.

7. Look at the early church fathers starting on page 12. Ask the group to list the names, who they were, and what they communicated about the deity of Christ:
   a. Ignatius
   b. Polycarp of Smyrna
   c. Justin Martyr
   d. Irenaeus

8. On pages 14–17, Dr. Lutzer writes about the early Christians and their view of the lordship, the deity of Christ. Take a minute to imagine what it might be like to be asked to give homage to Caesar only once per year.
   a. Would you do this? Why or why not?
   b. How would your decision be different if you had a family with young children?

9. From pages 22–24, compile the list of Gnostic beliefs that Dr. Lutzer presents in the text:
   a. A religious movement
   b. Could not tolerate exclusive claims made by Jesus Christ
   c. Similar to modern day quest of spirituality (how so?)
   d. Our need is not for forgiveness, but for enlightenment
   e. Jesus is not necessary for salvation
   f. Each person can encounter God in their own way
   g. More from other pages?

F. Biblical Study (optional): 30 minutes

DISCUSSION QUESTIONS

This section is designed for biblical study of related passages in small groups.

1. Review these passages. What do they say about the lordship and deity of Christ? What are the implications of these passages?
   a. 1 Peter 3:15
   b. 2 Peter 1:2

2. Together in your small groups, read through the following passages and write down what each says about the doctrine of the nature of Christ (Christology):
   a. Matthew 16:16
   b. Mark 8:29
   c. Luke 9:20
   d. John 1:1
   e. Romans 9:5
   f. Philippians 2:5–11
   g. Colossians 1:16
   h. Hebrews 1:8
   i. 1 John 4:2–3

3. As you read through the verses, what are the implications for:

    a. Those also included in the text?

    b. The reader?

    c. You, today in the twenty-first century?

4. What encouragement do you find in reading these verses? Share this with your group.

SPECIAL EXERCISE

Review the Nicene Creed. What strikes you about the words that are used? On what texts in Scripture are these tenets based? Work as a small group to find the Scripture verses that speak to each statement of faith.

G. Message: 10–12 minutes

After the small group discussions, say something like this:

In *The Da Vinci Deception* we see a short narrative of Constantine and his rise to power, a vision of the cross of Christ, and subsequent conquering under the name and symbol of the Cross. He subsequently established amnesty of Christians in the kingdom with the Edict of Milan. He then assumed an active role in the doctrinal debates of the day; his primary concern was that of unity in the kingdom (pp. 5–6).

According to Brown and his research, the Council of Nicaea was called to establish the canon of Scripture that we now know as the New Testament. According to the legend, at this meeting, the books were chosen that most represented the ultimate goals of a sexist, chauvinistic sect of Christianity.

Actually, the debate at Nicaea was a passionate discussion about one letter in a Greek word that could change the entire landscape of Christian doctrine with implications for the salvation of man. It is not often that we get into debates over words. We often assume we know what another person means when he or she talks with us, because we know the person or are familiar with how he or she talks. We know that the person says "pillow" funny or pronounces "root" and "foot" the same.

In the early church, when it came to matters of doctrine and theology, there was no room for this sort of lax interpretation in talking or writing. Theologians knew they had to be clear; they had to be precise. The minutia of difference in wording could have massive implications for the history of the church, or for what a word might communicate about God's grace, his love, his forgiveness, his very being. Constantine knew this; the bishops at Nicaea knew this. There was an imminent need to clarify any discrepancy between theologians.

An extension of this argument is present throughout the thesis of *The Da Vinci Code*. Brown's idea, promulgated by many others as well, that the Christ we know in the New Testament and the one we see in the Gnostic texts are two very different people, is cataclysmic. The idea that all religions are just variant paths on the way to [a] god is preposterous and by the very nature of communicating equality defeats the possibility that any are true. Jesus Christ is the way, or there is no way. In our doctrinal or theological discussions today, the one letter, the one small word can communicate an entirely opposite idea about God, about righteousness, about forgiveness and grace.

For Brown to assert that there is no truth to be known about Jesus (*The Da Vinci Code*, p. 342), that all religions are simply salve for the wounds of this world, is to assert a devastating blow to all of reality! In the face of real death, destruction, war, or cancer, what help is a mythical superstition about a man who came from heaven?

In the end, the iota does matter. The one small letter, the one distinctive separating of one word from another word that communicates far less, the letter that communicates truth versus a lie, is an important detail to know. In the same way, when we read the text of *The Da Vinci Code*, or any text written by people, we must understand the very truth of what is being debated. In a postmodern world that says truth cannot be really fully known, authors and readers will never really understand each other because words have different meanings.

We must rush in to decipher the truth about what we are reading: What happened at Nicaea? Who was Jesus? What does Jesus mean to me? Is the church really deceptive, murderous, and conniving? Is the God of the Old Testament different from the God of the New? Is he really hidden, keeping himself from us, and only a select few may find their inner spark? Has God revealed himself to people? Does he want to be known? Has he provided a way of salvation for sinful men or not?

These are questions we must have solid answers to; they are the only questions worth asking and worth answering.

Conclude in prayer for your group.

H. Homework (optional): 5 minutes

As participants are able, encourage them to do a little work outside of your regular session time.
1. Reading for this week: Chapter Two: "That Other Bible"
   a. Underline and mark up the book as you read.
   b. Write down any questions you have as you come across the material.
   c. Read through the text with your Bible at the ready, looking up verses and reading Scripture in response and in addition to what is in the Dr. Lutzer book.
2. Do some outside research on your own—look up on the Web or in newspaper articles what others are saying about *The Da Vinci Code*.
3. Have participants research the Gnostic Gospels for next week. Have each member bring in an article or review to share with his or her small group.

I. Handouts and Worksheets: 5 minutes

Have several copies of the handouts to give to your group participants this week. Everyone should take these materials home and engage with them during the time between sessions. It will help foster comprehension of the text.

CHAPTER QUIZ (p. 87)

1. According to *The Da Vinci Code*, what happened at the Council of Nicaea? pp. 1–2
2. According to Brown's book, why did Constantine call the meeting? pp. 1–2
3. When did the Council of Nicaea meet? p. 1
4. In what modern country is Nicaea? p. 4
5. In actuality, the Council of Nicaea was convened to refute whom? Why? pp. 5–6
6. What are the implications of this early theologian's views? pp. 7–8
7. Who are three of the four theologians that Dr. Lutzer names who embraced the deity of Christ before the council ever met? pp. 12–13
8. List at least two passages in the New Testament that declare the divinity of Christ. p. 7
9. What Roman structure was mentioned in the chapter? What was its significance? pp. 15–16
10. What heresy is alluded to in the first chapter? What are some of its claims? pp. 17–18

CHAPTER SUMMARY (p. 88)

The chapter opens with the account of Constantine, who, in his desire to overthrow Rome, had a vision of the cross of Christ and was told in the vision to conquer under the banner of the Cross. He did so, overthrowing, conquering, and eventually establishing the Edict of Milan, which offered freedom of religion for Christians. In addition, knowing the passion that theologians had for right doctrine, he issued a decree that the bishops meet to clarify what Scripture says about Christ and his deity. Arius had been promoting a doctrine that stripped Jesus of his deity, making him more than a man but not God. The ecumenical council met in Nicaea to establish the doctrine of Christ. Arius was declared a heretic, and the doctrine was secured by the bishops, using the Greek term *homoousius* to communicate the deity of Christ. *The Da Vinci Code* is wrong in asserting that Constantine fabricated the deity of Christ to give him more power.

Dr. Lutzer continues to develop the argument that Jesus' deity was secure before the ecumenical council, and that meeting was simply a formality to halt more arguing among orthodox Christians. Dr. Lutzer calls the witness of the church fathers including Polycarp, Justin Martyr, Irenaeus, and Tertullian who embraced the deity of Christ long before the council met. Dr. Lutzer continues by showing support from the early church, the martyrs who were killed for declaring the lordship and deity of Christ under pain of death. They were required once a year to submit homage to Caesar as lord, as a god. Martyrs did not submit to this authority, so they were in effect declaring the lordship and deity of Christ.

The Da Vinci Code also claims that the council meeting at Nicaea was an act to codify the canon of the New Testament, compiling books that raised men above women, securing the power of the male-dominated church, to hide the truth about Jesus' marriage to Mary, and to secure their stance of sexual repression. This stands in opposition to the "truths" expressed in the Gnostic Gospels that raise up the divine feminine, sexual purification rites, and propose that Jesus and Mary were married and had a child.

Here are a few implications from the chapter:

1. The testimony of the council was that the deity had already been agreed upon before the meeting, not determined at the meeting.

2. Other major church fathers had already embraced the deity of Christ.

3. Early Christians were willing to die or be persecuted for the deity of Christ because they knew the truth.

4. The deity of Christ is essential for the salvation of men and women.

5. The Gnostic heresy has existed throughout history and still exists today in books like *The Da Vinci Code* and the Gnostic Bible.

PERSONAL RESPONSE (p. 89)

1. Review the Nicene Creed and meditate on the descriptions in the texts. Is this the faith that you profess?

2. Spend time looking up verses for each of the tenets set forth in the Creed:

> **The Nicene Creed**
>
> *I believe in one God, the Father Almighty, Maker of heaven and earth, and of all things visible and invisible.*
>
> *And in one Lord Jesus Christ, the only-begotten Son of God, begotten of the Father before all worlds; God of God, Light of Light, very God of very God; begotten, not made, being of one substance with the Father, by whom all things were made.*
>
> *Who, for us men for our salvation, came down from heaven, and was incarnate by the Holy Spirit of the virgin Mary, and was made man; and was crucified also for us under Pontius Pilate; He suffered and was buried; and the third day He rose again, according to the Scriptures; and ascended into heaven, and sits on the right hand of the Father; and He shall come again, with glory, to judge the quick and the dead; whose kingdom shall have no end.*
>
> *And I believe in the Holy Ghost, the Lord and Giver of Life; who proceeds from the Father and the Son; who with the Father and the Son together is worshipped and glorified; who spoke by the prophets.*
>
> *And I believe one holy catholic and apostolic Church. I acknowledge one baptism for the remission of sins; and I look for the resurrection of the dead, and the life of the world to come. Amen.*

3 In your circle of friends, with what in this creed would they have difficulty? Why?

4. Spend time in prayer for your family and friends who may be confused about the real Jesus, or who may have difficulty accepting the truths set forth in Scripture.

J. Other Resources (optional)

On the matter of the Council of Nicaea and Constantine, have students consider the following resources this week if they have time. Compare and contrast articles with one another and with Scripture.

1. Articles

    a. Ramsey, Sir William, *The Bearing of Recent Discovery on the Trustworthiness of the New Testament* (London: Hodder & Stoughton, 1915)

    b. *New Advent Catholic Encyclopedia* article on "Nicaea" (Robert Appleton Company, 1908)

2. Books
   a. The Gospel of John, New Testament
   b. Noll, Mark, *Turning Points* (Grand Rapids, MI: Baker Academic, 2000)
   c. Hordern, William E., *A Layman's Guide to Protestant Theology* (New York: The Macmillan Co., 1957)

3. Video/TV/Internet
   a. www.NewAdvent.org—Catholic Encyclopedia
   b. www.Wikipedia.org

SESSION THREE:
THAT OTHER BIBLE

Introduction

LESSON TEXT

Dr. Lutzer, Chapter Two: "That Other Bible"

LESSON KEY FOCUS/IDEA

The purpose of this session is to help students understand the nature of the Gnostic Gospels, their origin, their dating, their contents, and their threat to Christianity.

LESSON GOALS

As a result of this session, participants will:

1. Learn the history and contents of the Gnostic Gospels.
2. Realize the implications of the theology presented in the Gnostic Gospels.
3. Understand how New Testament author Luke researched the life of Christ.

LESSON MATERIALS

The Da Vinci Deception books, Bibles, pens, paper, handouts, small group questions, DVD

LESSON FORMAT

A. Welcome	3–5 minutes
B. Opening Activities (optional)	5–10 minutes
C. Intro to DVD	2 minutes
D. DVD Segment	6 minutes
E. DVD Segment Recap (optional)	10 minutes
F. Small Group Discussion	30 minutes
G. Biblical Study (optional)	30 minutes
H. Message	12–15 minutes
I. Personal Application/Response (optional)	15 minutes
J. Homework	3–5 minutes
K. Handouts and Worksheets	3–5 minutes
a. Chapter Quiz	
b. Chapter Summary	
c. Personal Response	
L. Other Resources (optional)	

A. Welcome: 3–5 minutes

1. Welcome everyone back, and greet new people who may have joined the group.

    2. Explain to participants why you are covering *The Da Vinci Deception* (from Author's Note, p. xiii).

        a. Investigate the historical roots of Christianity.

        b. Give credible answers to questions like these:

            i. Who is Jesus?

            ii. Is the New Testament a reliable source?

            iii. What should this mean to us in the twenty-first century?

    3. Review last week's material with the group—what was covered and what the group should have done to prepare for the session (see the previous lesson).

    4. Give a brief overview of what will be covered in this session. They will:

        a. Learn the history and contents of the Gnostic Gospels.

        b. Realize the implications of the theology presented in the Gnostic Gospels.

        c. Understand how New Testament author Luke researched the life of Christ.

B. Opening Activities (optional): 5–10 minutes

HISTORICAL QUIZ

Tell everyone to jump to their feet when they think they know the answer. Award 1000 points to the first person to jump if he or she has the correct answer. Take away 500 points for every wrong answer. Afterward, total the points and give a prize(s) to the winner(s).

    In what year:

1. Did Columbus discover the Americas? (Answer: *1492*)
2. Was the Magna Carta signed? (Answer: *1215—the first signing*)
3. Did World War I begin? (Answer: *1914*)
4. Did World War II end? (Answer: *1945*)
5. Was the U.S. Constitution ratified? (Answer: *1789*)
6. Was the War of 1812? (Answer: *1812*)
7. Was JFK shot? (Answer: *1963*)
8. Extra 1000 points for the date! (Answer: *November 22*)
9. Was former president Bill Clinton born? (Answer: *1946*)
10. Extra 2000 points for the date! (Answer: *August 19*)
11. Was Jesus born? (Answer: *4 BC*)
12. Add others as interest and time allow.

BREAKTHROUGH

Divide into groups and give each group paper and a pen or pencil. Explain that each group is a research and development department of a major corporation. Their assignment is to design a *fantastic breakthrough* product for the category that you will give them. They should brainstorm ideas and be ready to report to the whole group. Give each group one of the following product categories: automobile, kitchen, computer, television, airplane, camera, and college.

After a few minutes, have the groups report what they designed. Then ask the whole group to brainstorm how they would design and market a new and improved man and/or woman.

C. Intro to DVD: 2 minutes

Preview the DVD and prepare the group with questions to think about as they watch the segment. Share with the group what the DVD segment will cover and how it will coincide with Dr. Lutzer's book.

Questions you want the participants to address:

1.

2.

3.

D. DVD Segment: 6 minutes

Watch the DVD segment together. Divide into small groups afterwards to work through the material supplied for the small group leaders, page 28–29.

E. DVD Segment Recap (optional): 10 minutes

Use these questions to discuss the video segment:

1. When have you heard anything like this before? Where?
2. How does this compare with what you have grown up understanding?
3. What is your response to what you just heard?
4. What are the dangers associated with this material?

F. Small Group Discussion: 30 minutes

SMALL GROUP LEADER NOTES

Make sure that your small group leaders have copies of the necessary handouts for the session. Remember that the purpose of the small group discussions is to help members interact with the material on a personal level, to encourage members to share their experiences and their responses, and to study together.

SMALL GROUP LEADER HELPS

1. Small groups should be safe places to discuss and interact with the material. So . . .
   a. Don't monopolize the conversations or allow a group member to do so.
   b. Ask open-ended questions:
      i. How might someone respond to what Dr. Lutzer said?
      ii. How might you interact with others who have read the book?
      iii. What concerns do you have based on what you have read or seen?
      iv. What Bible verses relate directly to what we are reading and hearing?
2. Prepare in advance so you have additional material or questions.
3. Incorporate material from both the book and the video segments.
4. Small groups should be a place to discuss the Bible together.
5. Small groups should be where God works in people's lives, so be sure to take a moment at the end to pray for how you can use the material to interact with peers, friends, and family.

PRELIMINARY SMALL GROUP DISCUSSION QUESTIONS

1. What is the Gnostic Bible, and what is its attraction for readers? (Answer: *The Gnostic Bible contains writings discovered in 1945 that were not part of the official canon. It appeals to modern readers because it promotes tolerance, do-it-yourself religion, and a pro-feminist viewpoint.*)
2. How does the Gnostic version of Christianity differ from the Christianity of the Bible? (Answer: *It portrays a pro-feminist, androgynous God, sexual rituals, and teachings of Jesus that are unlike anything else in the Bible.*)
3. Is the Gnostic Bible as reliable as the Bible? (Answer: *No. The Gnostic Bible is not supported by history, sequential events, or archeology, actual locations, etc. It was not written by eyewitnesses, as the four official Gospels were. The Bible stands up to scrutiny, while the Gnostic Bible does not.*)
4. What did the Gnostics believe? (Answer: *They believed that there was hidden knowledge secret to everyone but themselves; that God was both male and female; that there were sexual rituals appropriate to Christianity; that the original church was matriarchal and feminine.*)
5. Why are those beliefs so popular today? (Answer: *Our modern culture supports doctrinal diversity, "tolerance," feminism, and experiencing God in ways other than through Christ.*)

ADDITIONAL SMALL GROUP DISCUSSION QUESTIONS

1. Dr. Lutzer explains that the Gnostic Gospel presents an alternate way of being Christian (p. 25–26).
   a. What you think it means to be a Christian?
   b. Share your concerns with the group about a "religion" or "spirituality" that piggybacks on Christianity.
2. In America, what is another understanding of what it means to be Christian?
3. What does Scripture say it takes in order to be considered a Christian? Look up the verses and write out what each verse says about humanity and the way of salvation.

a. John 1:12

b. John 3:16

c. Romans 3:23

d. Romans 3:24

e. Romans 5:8

f. Romans 6:23

g. Romans 10:9–10

h. Romans 10:13

i. 1 John 1:9

4. What other passages communicate our need for a Savior? Check out these.

 a. 2 Corinthians 5:17

 b. Ephesians 2:8–9

5. Ask one or two people to share the Gospel of Christ with the group. These will be brave people, perhaps even the group leader.

 a. This does not have to be the story of salvation; for example, it might be just the recounting of the life of Christ.

 b. Have the rest of the group ask questions or share in response:

 i. What would they have included in the sharing?

 ii. What would they have left out?

 iii. What is the most important element to include?

 iv. What are some elements that we usually leave out as Christians? Details that are important?

OPTIONAL SMALL GROUP ACTIVITY

Last week part of the homework was to research the Gnostic Gospels and bring an article or review of the texts. Take some time to share the findings within your small groups. Groups may only have time for one or two individuals to share and discuss. Discussion questions may include these:

1. What is the tone of the article you are reading? Supportive, critical, apprehensive?

2. How does what you are reading sound similar to the Holy Bible?

3. How does what you are reading sound different?

4. What is a sound biblical response to what you are reading?

5. Support your findings with Scripture.

G. Biblical Study (optional): 30 minutes

After the preliminary small group discussions and activities, consider using the following as a small group Bible study before launching into the session's message.

Read the following passages in your small groups, then work through the questions that follow.

2 TIMOTHY 3:14–17

[14] But you must remain faithful to the things you have been taught. You know they are true, for you know you can trust those who taught you. [15] You have been taught the holy Scriptures from childhood, and they have given you the wisdom to receive the salvation that comes by trusting in Christ Jesus. [16] All Scripture was inspired by God and is useful to teach us what is true and to make us realize what is wrong in our lives. It corrects us when we are wrong and teaches us to do what is right. [17] God uses it to prepare and equip his people to do every good work.

2 PETER 1:19–21

[19] Because of that experience, we have even greater confidence in the message proclaimed by the prophets. You must pay close attention to what they wrote, for their words are like a lamp shining in a dark place—until the Day dawns, and Christ the Morning Star shines in your hearts. [20] Above all, you must realize that no prophecy in Scripture ever came from the prophet's own understanding, [21] or from human initiative. No, those prophets were moved by the Holy Spirit, and they spoke from God.

DISCUSSION QUESTIONS

1. To what does the term "holy Scriptures" refer? (Answer: *The Old Testament primarily, with some New Testament letters that were considered inspired.*)
2. In 2 Timothy 3:15, what are the holy Scriptures able to do for Timothy and the reader?
3. Considering both passages, of what use are the holy Scriptures? List them and explain with a few more words what each means.
    a. Teaching:

    b. Rebuking:

    c. Correcting:

    d. Training:

    e. Equipping:

    f. Light in a dark place:

4. Look at the context of the 2 Timothy passage. Paul exhorts Timothy to do what? (v. 14)
    a. What is this in response to?
    b. How does this passage explicitly relate to where we are today?
5. In 2 Timothy 3:17, what does it mean to be thoroughly equipped for every good work?
6. What confidence can be found in 2 Peter 1:20–21?
7. When you leave this session, what encouragement or strength can you find in these passages?

H. Message: 12–15 minutes

Say something like this:

"Adam and Eve were not the first people, the nature of man is good, Scripture is not infallible, Jesus is one of the ways, all religions are paths to God, reincarnation is in the Bible, the resurrection is a personal spiritual awakening, and the error of eternal damnation are all carefully and lovingly revealed in the life and sayings of Jesus." (From a review of *The Mystic Christ* by Ethan Walter III.)

If someone had shared that quote with you, you could respond in a few ways. Perhaps your gut response would be, "No way, I can't believe that is in there—but it may be . . . the Bible is pretty big and I have not read all of it!" Maybe your response would be, "Absolutely not, I am sure of this, there is no way that any of those things are in Scripture. To say any of those things is to compromise the integrity of salvation and the holiness of God."

But maybe some of you are not quite sure. You have heard little phrases like this for some time; you have read *The Da Vinci Code*; you have seen articles and newscasts; you may have friends who say similar things. You may even feel that it must be true because you believe that Jesus cannot possibly be the only way to heaven. You may feel it has to be true because you feel those around you have never really given you the full scoop. The Holy Bible and its claims seem just a little too steep to believe; the stories seem like fairy-tales; the God seems too good; the people seem too bad for you to embrace what Scripture is saying. And so reading this quote and reading *The Da Vinci Code* seem to affirm some of your doubts. What you have read in the book, what you hear people saying around you seems more plausible.

If you are questioning and if you are struggling with some of these truths about the Bible, God, Jesus, his alleged marriage to Mary and their child, I'm glad that you are here to explore the truth. In our sessions we will confront the truth and errors that exist about the nature of these issues. I hope and pray that you will be encouraged and assured as we read through Scripture, as we watch videos, as we get to know each other, and as we study and pray together.

The reliability and inspiration of Scripture is important for us to understand. In 2 Timothy we can see Paul illustrating the sanctity and reliability of Scripture:

[14] But you must remain faithful to the things you have been taught. You know they are true, for you know you can trust those who taught you. [15] You have been taught the holy Scriptures from childhood, and they have given you the wisdom to receive the salvation that comes by trusting in Christ Jesus. [16] All Scripture is inspired by God and is useful to teach us what is true and to make us realize what is wrong in our lives. It corrects us when we are wrong and teaches us to do what is right. [17] God uses it to prepare and equip his people to do every good work.

And again in 2 Peter 1:19–21:

[19] Because of that experience, we have even greater confidence in the message proclaimed by the prophets. You must pay close attention to what they wrote, for their words are like a lamp shining in a dark place—until the Day dawns, and Christ the Morning Star shines in your hearts. [20] Above all, you must

realize that no prophecy in Scripture ever came from the prophet's own understanding, [21] *or from human initiative. No, those prophets were moved by the Holy Spirit, and they spoke from God.*

What we see and know is the integrity of Scripture is not based on the work of human beings; it is not built on committees that spend lots of thought and effort into "getting it right." Just as the Scriptures were inspired by the Holy Spirit, the leading of God, so the compilation of those Scriptures is secure because of the work of the Holy Spirit. We can know with certainty that the words of God as found in the Bible are excellent for building up the church, for revealing truth, and for disclosing the plan of salvation for people.

As we continue to work through materials surrounding *The Da Vinci Code*—materials that may be sensational or antagonistic—let's remind one another what we have been given. Let's encourage one another to remember the faith and tradition that we have known. Let us remember to stay grounded in the truths that we have known and to study and evaluate new information in light of the information that we already know to be true, trusting those who have gone before, trusting the infallible truths found in Scripture.

Conclude the discussion in prayer.

I. Personal Application/Response (optional): 15 minutes

1. Spend time in silent meditation on this material, allowing space and quiet to hear the voice of God.
   a. In what ways have you limited the scope of Jesus' claims to lordship, divinity, humanity?
   b. In what ways have you allowed the buzz of life instead of Scripture to construct your thinking?
   c. Do you have doubts about the claims that Christ has made or the account of those claims as expressed in the Old and New Testaments?
   d. Are your friends Christians? Or do they tend toward Gnostic thought, saying that there are multiple ways to God?
   e. How do you respond to this?
   f. How have you talked with them about this issue?
   g. How would you talk with them about this issue now?
2. Read pages 48–50 in Dr. Lutzer's book.
   a. What is your response to the Elaine Pagel's quote from the *Time* magazine article? How does it "sit with you"?
   b. How might you respond to someone who shared this thought with you personally?
3. Pray for those who are deceived by false teaching and are caught in the rush of twenty-first century spirituality. Pray that the Holy Spirit will move in their lives and reveal their error and confusion, allowing them to see the true Christ in Scripture.
4. Consider memorizing the passages that you discussed in your small group.

J. Homework: 5 minutes

As participants are able, encourage them to do a little work outside of your regular session time, with the following assignments:

1. Research the Gnostic Gospels with a new understanding and clarity as to what they are about.
   a. What are overt fallacies that you see?
   b. What questions do these "gospels" raise for Christians? For non-Christians?
2. Answer these questions as best as you are able with supporting texts:
   a. According to Gnosticism, what makes a person saved?
   b. According to Christianity, what makes a person saved?
3. Read Dr. Lutzer, Chapter Three: "Jesus, Mary Magdalene, and the Search for the Holy Grail."
   a. Underline and mark up the book as you read.
   b. Write down any questions you have as you come across the material.
   c. Read with your Bible at the ready, looking up verses and reading Scripture in response and addition to what is in the Dr. Lutzer book.
4. Do some outside research on your own by checking on the Web or in newspaper articles what others are saying about *The Da Vinci Code*.

K. Handouts and Worksheets: 5 minutes

Have several copies of the handouts to distribute to participants.
   1. Chapter Quiz
   2. Chapter Summary
   3. Personal Response

CHAPTER QUIZ (p. 90)
   1. Which of the following is *not* in the Gnostic Bible: (Answer: *The Gospel of Mark*)
      a. The Gospel of Mary
      b. The Gospel of Philip
      c. The Gospel of Thomas
      d. The Gospel of Mark
   2. In what Gnostic Gospel is the reference to the marriage of Jesus and Mary Magdalene? (Answer: *The Gospel of Philip*)
   3. Gnostic comes from what Greek word? Meaning what? (Answer: gnosis *meaning "knowledge"*)
   4. When and where were the Gnostic Gospels found? (Answer: *1945, in Egypt*)
   5. In what language were the Gnostic Gospels written? (Answer: *Coptic*)
   6. What does "spurious authorship" mean? (Answer: *Someone purported to be the author who isn't*—see pp. 34–35)

7. The Apocrypha is part of the Gnostic Bible—True or False. (Answer: *false*—see p. 41)

8. In *The Da Vinci Deception*, whose account is shown to be a reliable witness to the life of Jesus? (Answer: *Luke*—see p. 44)

CHAPTER SUMMARY (p. 91)

This chapter is Dr. Lutzer's response to the Gnostic Gospels, which are addressed frequently in Brown's book *The Da Vinci Code*, as being a more accurate and complete representation of the historical Jesus. Dr. Lutzer responds to the assertion that these new "gospels" are more reliable with an argument that includes late dates, spurious authorships, and the revelation of the cryptic, nonsensical teachings included in the books.

Dr. Lutzer opens the chapter with a quick overview of the definition of Gnosticism (from the Greek word *gnosis*: meaning "knowledge"), and the philosophical roots in Platonic thought and ideas that matter is evil. This implies that God would never have become human because to do so, he would become evil.

In the meat of the chapter, Dr. Lutzer recounts the history of the documents, most importantly their late dates—removed from the life of Christ by nearly twice the amount of time as the New Testament Gospels. Also included in this recounting is the spurious authorship where authors of the Gnostic texts would attach known apostles to the letters to give them credibility. Finally, Dr. Lutzer draws our attention to the conflicting and obscure ideas presented in the teachings of the Gnostic Gospels, giving examples for the reader to view.

In the last half of the chapter, Dr. Lutzer develops the idea that sometimes history can be written to bolster psychological or political ideals. Dr. Lutzer cites other historians, Raymond Brown (no relation to Dan Brown) and Andrew Greeley, who disagree with the accuracy, validity, and helpfulness of the Gnostic Gospels. In contrast, Dr. Lutzer shows us the historian and doctor Luke of the New Testament who undertook the effort to compile an historical record for Theophilus.

Dr. Lutzer closes the chapter with a call to response from the reader. Declaring that we have a choice to accept the teachings of the New Testament or the convoluted teachings of self-seeking Gnostic spirituality, Dr. Lutzer bids the reader to choose the narrow gate, the way that clearly and ultimately separates Christianity from Gnosticism as the only path to salvation.

PERSONAL RESPONSE (p. 92)

Review the material in the Personal Response section and provide copies for the participants.

L. Other Resources (optional)

Consider the following resources this week if you have time:

1. Articles to consider:
    a. Van Biema, David. "The Lost Gospels," *Time* (22 December 2003): 56.
    b. book reviews on the Gnostic Gospels
    c. short articles on the Gnostic spirituality

2. Books to consider:
    a. Barnstone and Meyers, eds., *The Gnostic Bible*
    b. Pagels, Elaine. *Beyond Belief*
    c. Borg, Marcus. *The Heart of Christianity*

3. Terms or ideas to look up and understand:
    a. The Nag Hammadi Library
    b. Gnosticism
    c. Early Church Heresies
        i. Docetism
        ii. Dualism

SESSION FOUR:
JESUS, MARY MAGDALENE, AND THE SEARCH FOR THE HOLY GRAIL

Introduction

LESSON TEXT

Dr. Lutzer, Chapter Three: "Jesus, Mary Magdalene, and the Search for the Holy Grail"

LESSON KEY FOCUS/IDEA

The purpose of this lesson is to respond to Brown's allegation in *The Da Vinci Code* that Leonardo da Vinci hid secret messages in the painting of *The Last Supper*, which communicate that the Holy Grail (the cup used at the last supper) is actually not a cup but Mary Magdalene, the wife of Jesus.

LESSON GOALS

As a result of this session participants will:

1. Learn the legend behind Mary Magdalene.
2. Know the truth about Mary Magdalene.
3. Discover what the New Testament reveals about Jesus and marriage.

LESSON MATERIALS

The Da Vinci Deception books, Bibles, pens, paper, handouts, small group questions, DVD, copies of *The Last Supper* by Leonardo da Vinci, a *Life Application New Testament Commentary*, a *Life Application Bible/NLT*

LESSON FORMAT

A. Welcome	3–5 minutes
B. Opening Activities (optional)	5–10 minutes
C. Intro to DVD	2 minutes
D. DVD segment	6 minutes
E. Small Group Discussion	30 minutes
F. Biblical Study (optional)	30 minutes
G. Message	10–12 minutes
H. Homework (optional)	5 minutes
I. Handouts and Worksheets	5 minutes
a. Chapter Quiz	
b. Chapter Summary	
c. Personal Response	
J. Other Resources (optional)	

A. Welcome: 3–5 minutes

1. Welcome everyone back and greet new people who may have joined the group.
2. Explain to participants why you are covering *The Da Vinci Deception* (from Author's Note, p. xiii).
   a. Investigate the historical roots of Christianity:
   b. Give credible answers to questions like these:
      i. Who is Jesus?
      ii. Is the New Testament a reliable source?
      iii. What should this mean to us in the twenty-first century?
3. Review last week's material with the group—what was covered and what the group should have done to prepare for the session (see the previous lesson).
4. Give a brief overview of what will be covered in this session. They will:
   a. Learn the legend behind Mary Magdalene.
   b. Know the truth about Mary Magdalene.
   c. Discover what the New Testament reveals about Jesus and marriage.

B. Opening Activities (optional): 5–10 minutes

Mary, Mary

Hand out paper and pens. Ask how many Marys the group thinks are mentioned in the Bible. Then see who can list them and one or more references for each in six minutes. Give a prize to whoever completes the task first, or to whoever has the most names and references. Here are the answers:

1. Mary the wife of Cleopas (Matthew 28:1: 27:56; Mark 15:40; John 19:25)
2. Mary of Magdala (Magdalene) (Luke 8:2 and elsewhere)
3. Mary the sister of Martha and Lazarus (Luke 10 and elsewhere)
4. Mary the mother of John Mark (Acts 12:12)
5. Mary in the church in Rome (Romans 16:6)
6. Mary the mother of Jesus (multiple)
7. Naomi was also known as Mara (Mary) (Ruth 1:20)

In Tune with Mary

Distribute paper and pens. At your signal, everyone should list secular songs with Mary in the title or chorus. Some examples follow:

1. "Proud Mary"—Creedence Clearwater Revival, Elvis, Tom Jones
2. "Little Mary"—Fats Domino
3. "Take a Message to Mary"—The Everly Brothers
4. "Hello Mary Lou"—Ricky Nelson
5. "What Will Mary Say"—Johnny Mathis
6. "Mary Had a Little Lamb"—child's song

7. "Last Dance with Mary Jane"—Tom Petty

8. "Mary, Don't Cry"—Stonewall Jackson

9. "Mary, Mary"—Run DMC

10. More . . .

Give a prize to the winner.

C. Intro to DVD: 2 minutes

Preview the DVD and prepare the group with questions to think about as they watch the segment. Explain what the DVD segment will cover and how it matches Dr. Lutzer's book.

Questions you want the participants to address:

1.

2.

3.

D. DVD Segment: 6 minutes

Watch the DVD segment together. Divide into small groups afterward to work through the material supplied for the small group leaders on page 39–41.

E. Small Group Discussion: 30 minutes

SMALL GROUP LEADER NOTES

Make sure that your small group leaders have copies of the necessary handouts for the session.

Remember that the purpose of the small group discussions is to help members interact with the material on a personal level, to encourage members to share their experiences and responses, and to study together.

SMALL GROUP LEADER HELPS

1. Small groups should be safe places to discuss and interact with the material. So . . .
   a. Don't monopolize the conversations or allow a group member to do so.
   b. Ask open-ended questions:
      i. How might someone respond to what Dr. Lutzer said?
      ii. How might you interact with those whom you know who have read the book?
      iii. What concerns do you have based on what you have read or seen?
      iv. What Bible verses relate directly to what we are reading/hearing?
2. Prepare in advance so you have additional material or questions.
3. Incorporate material from both the book and the video segments.
4. Small groups should be a place to discuss the Bible together.

5. Small groups should be where God works in people's lives, so be sure to take a moment at the end to pray about how you can use the material to interact with peers, friends, and family.

PRELIMINARY SMALL GROUP DISCUSSION QUESTIONS

1. What is the Priory of Sion, of which Leonardo da Vinci was purported to be a member? (Answer: *The Priory of Sion was "a small band of conspirators who knew the truth about the marriage of Jesus and Mary Magdalene, but because of opposition from the church, this explosive secret had to be hidden"* [see p. 51].)

2. According to *The Da Vinci Code*, how did Leonardo da Vinci supposedly carry out the work of the Priory? (Answer: *He worked secret coded images into his paintings.*)

3. What is the biblical evidence that Mary Magdalene was a harlot? (Answer: *There is none. This theory was speculation and in 1969 was corrected by the Vatican, which said that characterization was a misrepresentation.*)

4. Was Jesus a feminist? (Answer: *Jesus "broke with tradition in allowing women to travel with him and help support his ministry" (page 59). He treated women with more respect and honor than they traditionally received. But there is no evidence that he intended the church to be built on Mary, and there is direct evidence that he meant for it to be built on Peter—see also pp. 59–60.*)

5. What evidence does *The Da Vinci Code* use to support a marriage between Jesus and Mary Magdalene? Is this evidence credible? Why or why not? (Answer: *Some say that because Mary Magdalene touched Jesus after his resurrection, which only a married woman would do, they must have been married. This is not true because other women touched Jesus: "And as they went, Jesus met them and greeted them. And they ran to him, grasped his feet, and worshiped him." [Matthew 28:9]—see p. 63.*)

6. What reasons are there that Jesus could not have been married? (Answer: *He would have needed to marry someone as sinless as himself, which is impossible. Also, he needed to remain pure for his eventual marriage to his bride, the church.*)

ADDITIONAL SMALL GROUP DISCUSSION QUESTIONS

Finding Truth

1. Read Dr. Lutzer pp. 54–56 (starting with: "In his book, *Humanists and Reformers* . . ."). It discusses art historians' views of Brown's evaluation of *The Last Supper* and depictions in the painting. Does your opinion about the book change? Why or why not?

2. In regard to Brown's book, there is a lot of accusing and retaliation between Gnosticism and Christianity. Both seem to be able to respond to accusations with facts, with data that laypeople tend to accept as truth.
   a. On what basis do you as a reader and a student believe one source over another?
   b. What are your criteria for establishing truth?
   c. Who or what are your reliable sources for information?

3. What other information have we received from others, that we have not experienced firsthand, that we seem to believe without any qualms? For example . . .

    a. Concept of gravity

    b. Math

    c. Details of Pearl Harbor

    d. Family history

4. What might it take to convince of you otherwise of a truth that you have come to believe? Think, for example, of your family history, the atomic theory, the benefits of sleep and exercise, or something similar.

5. Describe a time when you were corrected from error or came to a realization of truth in your life.

F. Biblical Study (optional): 30 minutes

Turn to John 4:1–27. If you have a *Life Application New Testament Commentary*, supply your small group leaders with the textual notes from this passage. If you don't have this, use the notes from a *Life Application Bible/NLT*. They aren't as extensive but will help. The textual notes and information in these resources will be helpful in the following study.

    Have an individual read aloud the story of the Samaritan woman at the well.

DISCUSSION QUESTIONS:

1. Why is this story of the Samaritan woman significant to include in the Gospels?

2. What are the implications of Jesus walking through Samaria?

3. What are the implications of Jesus talking with the Samaritan woman and asking her to draw water for him? (Answer: *Jesus disregarded the stigma of associating with Samaritans. He also disregarded the accepted view of male superiority.*)

4. What truths does Jesus communicate to the woman at the well? (Answer: *The place of worship is not as significant as the heart of worship—John 4:23; the stigma that society puts on individuals is unimportant—John 4:9; the reality of value and forgiveness to a woman, and an adulteress—John 4:18; cultural taboos can be broken—John 4:27.*)

5. What do we learn about the character of Jesus?

6. What was Jesus' main concern in the passage?

7. How does this depiction of Jesus compare with the description of Jesus as a feminist?

8. How does this depiction of Jesus compare with the accusation that those who assembled the New Testament Scripture at Nicaea were women-hating, male chauvinists?

9. According to Dr. Lutzer's book, who are other women who traveled with Jesus? What Scriptures point to these women? (See p. 59.)

G. Message: 10–12 minutes

For your message, say something like the following:

Ultimately, at the base of every conversation, at the end of every day, at the heart of every gospel message is the story of Jesus redeeming people he loves. No story is more central in the Bible than that of God loving his people so much that he sent his Son to die a criminal's death for the sake of broken, sinful people. We need to know nothing more. Even Paul said that his goal was to know Christ crucified—1 Corinthians 2:1–5.

> *When I first came to you, dear brothers and sisters, I didn't use lofty words and impressive wisdom to tell you God's secret plan. ²For I decided that while I was with you I would forget everything except Jesus Christ, the one who was crucified. ³I came to you in weakness—timid and trembling. ⁴And my message and my preaching were very plain. Rather than using clever and persuasive speeches, I relied only on the power of the Holy Spirit. ⁵I did this so you would trust not in human wisdom but in the power of God.*

Thus we need to know the story well . . . to know the truth of the Gospel, and thus essentially the truth about Christ. In this chapter, as in most of the others included in Dr. Lutzer's book, our responsibility lies in seeking the truth of who Jesus Christ is. We need to research and know the Bible. We need to read reliable and trustworthy authors who are faithful to the traditions of our faith and to the teachings of the Word of God. And we must evaluate all the material that we see and hear, from articles to television programs, to movies, to the speaking of preachers and teachers in our churches. In all these places, we may be subject to sinful interpretation and fallible exposition of our great and Holy Redeemer. So let us pray and meditate on God's Word in order to recognize the lies when they come.

For centuries, books have deceived readers into believing they present an accurate representation of Christ, that they know Jesus best, that they understand, or that they have some hidden truth about the real Jesus. *The Da Vinci Code* is no different. It claims that there is a hidden knowledge about the Savior of the world. It claims to know the real version of history, what has been hidden, perverted, or changed to meet the needs of power mongers and sexists. *The Da Vinci Code* fits nicely into a twenty-first-century agenda of individual spirituality, of autonomous growth and study. It fits well into a time and place that does not tolerate a "religious right." It has no stomach for those that claim to know God and to know truth, when in fact our world says truth cannot be known except in one's own mind and heart.

What of Mary Magdalene and her marriage to Jesus? What of their love child, the marriage into the lineage of French royalty? Can we believe these statements? Can we believe that our Savior and his wife may have participated in sex rituals like pagans? In order to know, we need to establish a foundation on which we can build our theology and doctrine. If we start from a foundation that accepts documents like the Gnostic Gospels or the whim of an author, then we cannot be certain of the tenets of our faith, and we cannot be sure of our salvation, of God's goodness, or of God's holiness and power and, thus, of God's ability to save. We cannot be certain that what he says is truth, and that he will encourage and strengthen us in our time of need. We won't have confidence that Christ is for us and that the Holy Spirit illumines us.

When we see "new truths," let us run back to what we know to be certain, the old truths. Truth does not change. It cannot change, or it is simply not true. Looking back at the history of the church, Scripture has withstood the scrutiny of thousands of men and women attacking, critiquing, and questioning; yet it remains, it holds fast. In all the hundreds of years, greater things have challenged the church than Dan

Brown's assertions in *The Da Vinci Code*. It will stand again. Together as a church, a small group, a family, and an individiaul member of the body of Christ, we must remember that the true source of wisdom and power is God himself, and he has lovingly revealed himself to us in Scripture. Let us know that and rejoice.

H. Homework: 5 minutes

Encourage everyone to do a little work outside of your regular session time, with these suggestions:

1. Using a concordance, look up various women in the Bible, studying their relationship with Christ or how they fit into their respective communities.
    a. How do men view them?
    b. How does Jesus treat them?
    c. What is their understanding of the Messiah?
2. Read Dr. Lutzer, Chapter Four: "Banned from the Bible: Why?"
    a. Underline and mark up the book as you read.
    b. Write down any questions you have that arise from the material.
    c. Read with your Bible at the ready, looking up verses and reading Scripture in response and addition to what is in the Dr. Lutzer book.
3. Do some outside research on your own by checking on the Web or in newspaper articles what others are saying about *The Da Vinci Code*.

I. Handouts and Worksheets: 5 minutes

Have several copies of the handouts below to distribute to participants.

1. Chapter Quiz
2. Chapter Summary
3. Personal Response

CHAPTER QUIZ (p. 93)

1. In Mary's name, to what does Magdalene refer? (Answer: *Where she was from—her hometown.*)
2. What relationship does Mary have with Jesus according to New Testament Scriptures? (Answer: *Jesus cast out seven demons from her.*)
3. Who is named as responsible for slandering the name of Mary Magdalene? (Answer: *Pope Gregory, in AD 591*)
4. What was the name of the organization that was charged with protecting the information about the marriage between Jesus and Mary? (Answer: *The Priory of Sion*)
5. What Catholic organization directly opposed the above mentioned group? (Answer: *The Opus Dei*)
6. According to the art historians mentioned in Dr. Lutzer's book, what is their response to *The Da Vinci Code*'s view of *The Last Supper*? (Answer: *They view* The Last Supper *as a true Florentine depiction of betrayal and sacrifice.*)

7. Why was the Holy Grail so great a treasure for people to seek? (Answer: *It was believed to have magical powers.*)

8. What is the Sang Real? (Answer: *The Royal Line, in reference to the French Merovingians.*)

9. Referring to pp. 65–66 of Dr. Lutzer's book, what is the failure of the translation of the Gospel of Philip? (Answer: The Da Vinci Code *says that a word used for Mary is "spouse" of Jesus, that in actuality the text was initially in Coptic, not Aramaic, and that the text says nothing about marriage.*)

10. Does Dr. Lutzer believe the account of Philip is credible? Why or why not? (Answer: *No—the other material included in the text is cryptic and senseless.*)

11. Could Jesus have been married? Why or why not? (Answer: *No. Although marriage was acceptable and encouraged by Paul and others, Jesus would have had to marry someone as perfect as he—* pp. 74–76.)

CHAPTER SUMMARY (p. 94)

This chapter responds to the assertion in *The Da Vinci Code* that Jesus and Mary were, in fact, married and had a love child, perhaps with lineage extending to the present through French Royalty. It also responds to the view that Leonardo da Vinci painted *The Last Supper* with hidden secret images to communicate the truth about Jesus' relationship with Mary; that, in fact, she is the "Holy Grail," bearing the child of their love.

History tells us that Leonardo was born in the fifteenth century, painted under the masters, and felt the greatest calling was to paint. The church and images in Scripture inspired his paintings, even though history indicates that he had no true interest in the spiritual truths found in the Word. According to *The Da Vinci Code*, however, Leonardo was a passionate member of the Priory of Sion, an organization entrusted with keeping the truth about the marriage and child of Jesus and Mary hidden.

Dr. Lutzer then clarifies the Mary Magdalene as found in Scripture. The New Testament tells of seven "Marys." Dr. Lutzer corrects the view that Mary Magdalene was a prostitute, a view promulgated by Pope Gregory in the sixth century. We cannot know if she was a prostitute, and to assert it is to gossip and slander another believer in Christ. As Dr. Lutzer develops our understanding of Mary Magdalene, he also addresses the Gnostic view that Jesus had an intimate, if not sexual relationship with Mary, based on a single sketchy source—the Gospel of Philip.

The Da Vinci Deception reveals some of the teachings in the Gnostic Gospels about women in the church—that they should be preachers, that Jesus wanted to found the church on Mary, that Mary was anointed using a sex ritual. As Dr. Lutzer responds, believers should be confident that such a depiction of Jesus is completely false based on his other teachings about sexual purity in the body and the mind. We can see from Scripture that the way to connect with God is not through sexual rituals but through believing in the Lord Jesus Christ (Romans 10:9).

Closing the chapter, Dr. Lutzer addresses the possibility of Jesus' marriage. Could he have been married? Is it wrong to be married? From what we can see in the Bible, nothing is wrong with marriage. Paul celebrated marriage. Thus, if Jesus had, in fact, been married, would not Paul also have included a statement to that effect—saying that Jesus was married? Scripture *does* state that Jesus *will* be married. Throughout the New Testament, Jesus is called the "Bridegroom" and believers, who make up the church, are called his "bride." Christ has saved himself for us; he has made us his own. He has loved us, and he is our marriage partner for eternity.

PERSONAL RESPONSE (p. 95)

Sometime this week, skim the Gospels to review the interactions that Jesus had with women in first-century Palestine. As you scan the Scriptures, watching how Jesus spoke, healed, and welcomed these women, ask these questions:

1. How did Jesus reach the marginalized people of his day?
2. How did Jesus respond to the customs of his day? Why did he respond this way?
3. What encouragement can you find in seeing Jesus' responses?
4. How might Jesus' example apply to your relationships today?
   a. Are you marginalized? Are you being pushed aside?
   b. Are you turning your head from those around you who are not high class, beautiful, or rich?
5. What truths about Christ, about humanity, and about relationships can you see in the passages you have read?
6. What do you know to be certain about sinful nature and the need for a holy Redeemer?

J. Other Resources (optional)

Consider the following resources this week if you have time.

1. Articles to consider:
   a. Reardon, Patrick R. "*The Da Vinci Code* Unscrambled," *The Chicago Tribune*, sec. 5 (5 February 2004): 4.
   b. Bucher, Bruce. "Does *The Da Vinci Code* Crack Leonardo?" *The New York Times*, Arts and Leisure (2 August 2003).
2. Books to consider:
   a. The Gospel of Mary—the *Gnostic Bible*
   b. Picknett and Prince, *The Templar Revelation*, New York: Touchstone Books, Simon and Schuster, 1998.
3. Look up these terms or ideas to help understanding the book:
   a. Feminism.
   b. Mother Mary in the Roman Catholic tradition.
   c. Culture in first-century Palestine.

SESSION FIVE:
BANNED FROM THE BIBLE: WHY?

Introduction

LESSON TEXT

Dr. Lutzer, Chapter Four: "Banned from the Bible: Why?"

LESSON KEY FOCUS/IDEA

The purpose of this lesson is to inform participants how the New Testament canon was formed and on what basis various books were included or excluded from the New Testament that we have today.

LESSON GOALS

As a result of this session, participants will:

1. Learn about the ancient books not included in the New Testament canon.
2. Know the date and circumstances surrounding the closing of the New Testament canon.
3. Understand the criteria for selecting the books of the New Testament.

LESSON MATERIALS

The Da Vinci Deception books, Bibles, pens, paper, handouts, small group questions, DVD

LESSON FORMAT

A. Welcome	3–5 minutes	
B. Opening Activities (optional)	5–10 minutes	
C. Intro to DVD	2 minutes	
D. DVD Segment	6 minutes	
E. Small Group Discussion	30 minutes	
F. Message	10–12 minutes	
G. Personal Application (optional)	5–7 minutes	
H. Homework	3–5 minutes	
I. Handouts and Worksheets	2–3 minutes	
a. Chapter Quiz		
b. Chapter Summary		
c. Personal Response		
J. Other Resources (optional)		

A. Welcome: 3–5 minutes

1. Welcome everyone back, and greet new people who have joined the group.
2. Explain why you are covering *The Da Vinci Deception* (from Author's Note, p. xiii):
    a. To investigate the historical roots of Christianity.
    b. To give credible answers to questions like these:
        i. Who is Jesus?
        ii. Is the New Testament a reliable source?
        iii. What should this mean to us in the twenty-first century?
3. Review last week's material with the group—what was covered and what the group should have done to prepare for the session (see the previous lesson).
4. Present a brief overview of what the group will do at the current session. They will:
    a. Learn about the ancient books not included in the New Testament canon.
    b. Know the date and circumstances surrounding the closing of the New Testament canon.
    c. Understand the criteria for selecting the books of the New Testament.

B. Opening Activities (optional): 5–10 minutes

IN AND OUT

Have everyone stand. Explain that you want to select the chosen few who will continue on in the class. To do this, you make a series of statements. If a statement is true about them, they must sit down (or stand up if you so instruct). Tell those who are left standing that they may remain for the rest of the weeks that the class meets. You may add or subtract statements based on the people in your class.

- ♦ Sit down if someone drove you here.
- ♦ Sit down if you got a speeding ticket on the way here.
- ♦ Sit down if you are chewing gum.
- ♦ Stand up if you have never had a cavity.
- ♦ Stand up if you went to the dentist today.
- ♦ Sit down if at some time during the last month you locked yourself out of your house or car.
- ♦ Stand up if you have teenagers living at home.
- ♦ Sit down if a teenager in your house is presently grounded.
- ♦ Stand up if you did all of the assigned reading for this session.
- ♦ Sit down if you can't remember anything you read.
- ♦ Sit down if you are tired of standing up and sitting down.

Congratulate those few who are still standing and award them each a small prize, like a snack-size candy bar.

BIBLE BOOKS

Make copies of the list of "Bible Books" below with the instructions. (The correct answers follow.) Afterward, give the answers and award prizes to those with perfect papers.

Explain: Put these books of the Bible in correct order. Cross out any that do not belong. Do this from memory, without the use of a Bible or any other resource.

BIBLE BOOKS	**CORRECT ANSWERS**
Hezekiah	Genesis
Ezekiel	Leviticus
Obadiah	Deuteronomy
Malachi	1 Samuel
Genesis	2 Chronicles
Amos	Esther
Leviticus	Ecclesiastes
Zephaniah	Song of Songs
Habakkuk	Ezekiel
Jude	Amos
2 Peter	Obadiah
Colossians	Habakkuk
Romans	Zephaniah
Hesitations	Malachi
Deuteronomy	Romans
1 Samuel	Colossians
2 Chronicles	2 Peter
Song of Songs	Jude
Esther	Hezekiah (cross out)
Mical	Hesitations (cross out)
Ecclesiastes	Mical (cross out)

C. Intro to DVD: 2 minutes

Preview the DVD and prepare the group with questions to think about as they watch the segment. Explain what the DVD segment will cover and how it matches Dr. Lutzer's book.

Questions you want the participants to address:

1.

2.

3.

D. DVD Segment: 6 minutes

Watch the DVD segment together. Afterward, divide into small groups to work through the material supplied for the small group leaders on page 50–51.

E. Small Group Discussion: 30 minutes

SMALL GROUP LEADER NOTES

1. Make sure that your small group leaders have copies of the necessary handouts for the session.

2. Remember that the purpose of the small group discussions is to help members interact with the material on a personal level, to encourage members to share their experiences and their responses, and to study together.

SMALL GROUP LEADER HELPS

1. Small groups should be safe places to discuss and interact with the material. So . . .
   a. Don't monopolize the conversations or allow a group member to do so.
   b. Ask open-ended questions:
      i. How might someone respond to what Dr. Lutzer said?
      ii. How might you interact with others who have read the book?
      iii. What concerns do you have based on what you have read or seen?
      iv. What Bible verses relate directly to what we are reading/hearing?
2. Prepare in advance so you have additional material or questions.
3. Incorporate material from both the book and the video segments.
4. Small groups should be a place to discuss the Bible together.
5. Small groups should be where God works in people's lives, so be sure to take a moment at the end to pray for how you can use the material to interact with peers, friends, and family.

PRELIMINARY SMALL GROUP DISCUSSION QUESTIONS

1. Why were some books included in the biblical canon and others rejected? (Answer: *The books in the canon were collected, agreed upon, and accepted as the Word of God through divine providence. Most were written to local churches or individuals in the first century after Christ's death. Others were written for broader audiences. Some clues to authenticity: Was the author known or did he at least show acquaintance with apostolic thought? Was the author an eyewitness or did he hear directly from eyewitnesses? Is the book's content consistent with other Scripture?*)
2. How is it possible that a fallible church could choose an infallible set of books for the New Testament? (Answer: *The revelation and inspiration of God make this possible.*)
3. Read page 87–88 in Dr. Lutzer's book about the earliest copies of the letters that Paul and other authors penned. What significance do these circumstances imply about the importance and availability of the

letters? (Answer: *There would likely be few copies of the letters; they would be cherished; all the papers would be copied by hand; it would take a while for all the early churches to see and verify the letters.*)

4. Read the section on Marcion on p. 91. What implications would Marcion's rejection of Jews and biblical law have on the view of God, the New Testament doctrine of grace, and other tenets of Christianity? (Answer: *God would not demand justice and obedience to his law; there would be no opportunity for grace and mercy from the throne of God; the God of the Old Testament is not the same as the God of the New so grace means less, even nothing if there is no law that people are being called to uphold.*)

ADDITIONAL SMALL GROUP DISCUSSION QUESTIONS

Go through the book highlighting and reading the passages that are in the text. Read those passages to one another, exploring how they help support Dr. Lutzer's arguments.

1. From a spiritual perspective, looking solely at the doctrine of God, what do we know about his character; that is, what can we know for certain about the Scriptures that describe and reveal him? (Answer: *If we know that God is perfect and that he has revealed himself to people, we can be confident that he is at work securing the texts, letters, poems, and narratives that give us the perfect description of him as a holy God expecting reverence and obedience, and that he is merciful and forgiving.*)

2. Together explore a map of the Mediterranean world and Paul's missionary travel. Using the Bible, pinpoint the churches and regions that were addressed by the letters he sent.
    a. How many regions are covered by Paul's missionary journeys?
    b. What modern-day countries are included in these journeys?
    c. How many miles would Paul have traveled on these journeys?

F. Message: 10–12 minutes

For the message, say something like the following:

In a country where the Bible is commonplace, members of churches in the United States do not value the Holy Scriptures nearly enough. In many churches today, an epidemic of scriptural illiteracy can cause members to doubt, be confused, and even forget the simplest yet greatest promises that God has made to his people. As members of the body of Christ, as individuals loved by our Father in heaven, as people redeemed from our sinful state, we should know certain truths, facts, and figures about the Bible that will help us, encourage us, and enable us to be effective ministers of the gospel.

Not to burden anyone here with guilt or shame, and without raising your hands, answer these questions:

- ◆ **Do you know how many books of the Bible are in the Old Testament and New Testament?**
- ◆ **Have you memorized the order of the books of the Bible?**
- ◆ **Have you read through the Bible at least once?**

- ◆ Do you have a good idea of where significant narratives can be found (for example, the Fall, the stories of Abraham, Joseph, and Moses, the birth of Christ, the Beatitudes, the Crucifixion, promises regarding salvation, and so forth)?
- ◆ Have you memorized or can you find passages that talk about human sinful nature and about God's grace and salvation?
- ◆ Do you know the types of literature in Scripture: law, history, prophecy, poetry, epistles, etc.?

Some of us have memorized baseball stats, video game codes, phone numbers, or stock tickers and have read countless articles on investing and financing, how to raise children, how to maximize our workouts, and what health foods are rich in antioxidants, but we are negligent in our knowledge of Scripture. We don't know what the Bible says about how we should raise our children; we have no idea how we can be involved in the church. Many of us have more than five Bibles in our homes and don't use any of them with enough regularity to need several copies. At the same time, in various parts of the world, people soak up Scripture even though it is illegal to own a copy of God's Word.

In order to spot a fake $100 bill, FBI agents are not given counterfeited bills to study. Instead, agents who deal with counterfeiting are handed the originals, the actual printed bills from the U.S. Treasury, to study. They are expected to know what minute details to look for—marks, colors, and patterns—so that when they do see a counterfeit bill, they can immediately tell it is a fake. In the same way, we must know our Bibles; we must saturate and soak in the Word of God and the truth therein so when we hear accusations and questions, when we read counterfeit doctrine, we can immediately tell the false from the original.

Instead of passively hoping that we get our theology right or being caught up in fear or timidity when a book like *The Da Vinci Code* appears, if we actively seek the truth in God's Word, we can confront these fallacies, accusations, and heresies with the truth. We are glad you are here in order to explore the truths that can be known, that have been known for many centuries.

Consider the quote from Bernard Ramm (pp. 122–123): "A thousand times over, the death knell (slow bell ringing) of the Bible has sounded, the funeral procession formed, the inscription cut on the tombstone. . . ."

In light of the "new evidence" that has surfaced, and in light of the "evidence" that Brown presents in his book and which has appeared in heresies for centuries before, we find that truth remains. The church has lasted for centuries, the Holy Spirit has worked in the lives of countless men and women, and the truth of the gospel penetrates the deepest regimes and changes the darkest hearts, renewing them, redeeming them, saving them.

The Gnostic Gospels, the banned books, and the heresies that have crept along through the centuries have never taken hold. They have never overcome the power of the gospel or withstood the truths found in God's Word. Let us be confident in the work that has been done and find comfort and strength in those who have gone before us, not because they were good men and women, not because they were brave or well thought of or well educated, but in the fact that our God reigns. He lives, he has revealed himself, and he is working in the world.

G. Personal Application/Response (optional): 15 minutes

Part of the argument against the veracity of the Bible is that it has gone though so many revisions and languages that it can hardly be trusted as reliable or true. Get a copy of the *New Living Translation* of the Bible and read through the article at the front entitled "Introduction to the *New Living Translation*." Find the answers to the following questions:

1. What is the intent of the translation team?
2. What is the purpose of the translation?
3. What texts did the scholars use in the translation of the text?
4. What is a dynamic-equivalence translation?
5. What does this mean for the reader of the *New Living Translation*?
6. How is this "dynamic-equivalence" formed?
7. Who are the scholars who translated and reviewed the material?

If you have time, compare these notes with those of other popular translations such as the NIV, ESV, and NKJV.

1. What do you find in common?
2. Are there dissimilarities? If so, what are they?

Take some time this week to sit with your Bible. If you have access to more than one translation, consider setting them side by side and comparing them as you read a passage. Compare the date of publication, the publisher, the words used, the language style, tone, punctuation, etc., to get a grasp of the differences in translations and the reasons for these differences.

H. Homework: 5 minutes

Encourage everyone to do a little work outside of your regular session time, with these suggestions:

1. Read Dr. Lutzer, Chapter Five: "A Successful Search for Jesus."
2. Underline and mark up the book as you read.
3. Write down any questions you have that arise from the material.
4. Read with your Bible at the ready, looking up verses and reading Scripture in response and addition to what is in the Dr. Lutzer book.
5. Do some outside research on your own by checking on the Web or in newspaper articles what others are saying about *The Da Vinci Code*.
6. View a map of the Mediterranean world and Paul's missionary travel. Using Scripture, pinpoint the churches and regions that were addressed by the letters he sent.
   a. How many regions are covered by Paul's missionary journeys?
   b. What modern day countries are included in these journeys?
   c. Using the map's scale, approximately how many miles did Paul travel on these journeys?
7. Go through the personal response worksheet and spend time reviewing the validity of Scripture. Answer this question: How can we know that the Old and New Testaments are true and can be trusted?

8. Memorize the names of the books of the Bible, in order, during the course of this class.

9. List significant verses that may be useful when talking with peers, colleagues, and family about *The Da Vinci Code*.

I. Handouts and Worksheets: 5 minutes

Have several copies of the handouts to distribute to participants.

1. Chapter Quiz
2. Chapter Summary
3. Personal Response

CHAPTER QUIZ (p.96)

1. What does the word *canon* mean? (Answer: *General rule, principle or standard for measuring*)

2. Give three passages of Scripture that speak to the words in the Bible coming from God. (Answer: *Exodus 24:4; 2 Timothy 3:16–17; 2 Peter 1:19–21*)

3. What five books are included in the canon that "almost did not make it"? (Answer: *Song of Solomon, Ecclesiastes, Esther, Proverbs, Ezekiel—p. 84*)

4. According to Dr. Lutzer, we can be certain that the canon of the Old Testament was finalized when? (Answer: *About 400 BC*)

5. In what city was the canon of the Old Testament agreed upon? (Answer: *Jamnia AD 90—p. 86*)

6. When Paul refers to Scripture, what is he referring to? (Answer: *The Old Testament*)

7. What is the teaching of the apostles that was not included in the canon of the New Testament? (Answer: *The Didache*)

8. What were the criteria for acceptance into the New Testament canon? (Answer: *Apostolicity, conformity, acceptance*)

9. What happened at the Council of Hippo in AD 393? (Answer: *The ratification of the twenty-seven New Testament books*)

10. According to Dr. Lutzer, what is the problem with many Gnostic writings? (Answer: *Hybrid teachings, superstitions, foolish heresies—p. 100*)

CHAPTER SUMMARY

Dr. Lutzer's purpose in this chapter is to distinguish the books included in the New Testament canon from those not included and the reason(s) why and when these decisions were made and who, in fact, made these decisions. According to *The Da Vinci Code*, men who wanted to change the church into a patriarchal community put the New Testament together as an act of censorship. In the first few pages of the chapter, Dr. Lutzer gives the reader a quick overview of the rejected texts and excerpts from those texts. He also alludes to the program on the History Channel, *Banned from the Bible*, which is available on DVD.

Dr. Lutzer begins his argument for the canonicity of our Bible with the Old Testament, the Hebrew Scriptures. He gives several supporting texts of God's authorizing the texts that were being used in Jewish worship, including Exodus, Deuteronomy, Joshua, 1 Samuel, and Nehemiah. He clarifies that not all works circulating at the time were considered inspired. On p. 85, Dr. Lutzer states that the list of canonical Old Testament books was agreed upon by 400 BC and ratified at the Council of Jamnia in AD 90. These texts have been supported and alluded to by several New Testament figures including Paul, Luke, and Jesus himself.

The authority of the New Testament canon is also found in the authority of the character of God, not of human beings and committees. In the next section, Dr. Lutzer works through the development of the New Testament—to whom letters were written, how they were distributed, and how widely they were accepted and used. After the heretic Marcion began promoting his own list of "accepted" works, which opposed Jewish and biblical law, scholars in the early church formed their own list of authoritative books. This list is supported by other documents and the acceptance by the early church in its wide use of these texts. Ultimately these texts were affirmed by the Holy Spirit, as the church and its members were guided and they recognized the works that rightly communicate God's message to the people he loves.

Closing this chapter, Dr. Lutzer shows that the church was guided along in its selection of canonical Scriptures in the same way that each individual writer was led by the Spirit in the writing of the letters, narrative, law, or poetry. In the way that we accept the infallible writings of fallible men led by the Spirit, we also accept the infallible canon of Scripture as determined by the fallible church, as she was led by the Spirit. Dr. Lutzer concludes this chapter with a description of how the canon came to be.

PERSONAL RESPONSE (p. 98)

Review the material in the Personal Response section and provide copies for the participants.

J. Other Resources (optional)

Consider the following resources this week if you have time:

1. Books
   a. Wilson, Neil S. and Linda K. Taylor, eds. *Tyndale Handbook of Bible Charts and Maps*. Wheaton, IL: Tyndale House Publishers, 2001.
   b. *What the Bible Is All About: Reproducible Maps, Charts, Time Lines and Illustrations*. Ventura, CA: Regal Books, 1989.
   c. McDowell, Josh. *Evidence That Demands a Verdict*. Nashville, TN: Thomas Nelson Publishers, 1999.
2. Video/DVD
   a. A&E History Channel, *Banned from the Bible*, DVD, 2003.
2. Terms or ideas to look up and understand:
   a. Council of Hippo, AD 393
   b. Council of Jamnia, AD 90
   c. Canon of Scripture
   d. The Apocrypha

SESSION SIX:
A SUCCESSFUL SEARCH FOR JESUS

Introduction

LESSON TEXT

Dr. Lutzer, Chapter Five: "A Successful Search for Jesus"

LESSON KEY FOCUS/IDEA

The purpose of this session is to help the participants explore the true depiction of Jesus in Scripture and to learn how *The Da Vinci Code* undermines that true Jesus with supposed secret documents, conspiracies, and fabrications.

LESSON GOALS

As a result of this session, participants will:

1. Understand the current criticisms regarding the Jesus found in the New Testament.
2. See the evidence for Jesus as supported by the reliability of the New Testament record.
3. Discover the evidence for Jesus as supported by the disciples.
4. Learn the evidence for Jesus as supported by eyewitnesses.
5. Encounter the true Jesus of Scripture and what his life, death, and resurrection mean for people today.

LESSON MATERIALS

The Da Vinci Deception books, Bibles, pens, paper, handouts, small group questions, DVD

LESSON FORMAT

A. Welcome	3–5 minutes
B. Opening Activity (optional)	10–25 minutes
C. Intro to DVD	2 minutes
D. DVD segment	6 minutes
E. Small Group Discussion	30 minutes
F. Message	10–12 minutes
G. Personal Application (optional)	5 minutes
H. Homework	5 minutes in session
I. Handouts and Worksheets	5 minutes
a. Chapter Quiz	
b. Chapter Summary	
c. Personal Response	
J. Other Resources (optional)	

A. Welcome: 3–5 minutes

1. Welcome everyone back, and greet new people who have joined the group.
2. Explain why you are covering *The Da Vinci Deception* (from Author's Note, p. xiii):
    a. To investigate the historical roots of Christianity
    b. To give credible answers to questions like these:
        i. Who is Jesus?
        ii. Is the New Testament a reliable source?
        iii. What should this mean to us in the twenty-first century?
3. Review last week's material with the group—what was covered and what the group should have done to prepare for the session (see the previous lesson).
4. This would be a good time to check to see if they have any extra questions that arose in their reading or outside research.
    a. Review with participants the material for the evening, a preface of what will be covered in the chapter.
    b. Overview what the group will do at the current session. They will:
        i. Understand the current criticisms regarding the Jesus found in the New Testament.
        ii. See the evidence for Jesus as supported by the reliability of the New Testament record.
        iii. Discover the evidence for Jesus as supported by the disciples.
        iv. Learn the evidence for Jesus as supported by eyewitnesses.
        v. Encounter the true Jesus of Scripture and what his life, death, and resurrection mean for people today.

B. Opening Activity (optional): 10–25 minutes

THE TRUE JESUS

You may want to print out this quiz and distribute copies and pens. Otherwise, read the questions one at a time and have everyone write down their answers or give them verbally.

As an extra element, you could have individuals or groups find and read aloud the Scripture verses that apply to each statement.

1. Jesus was born in a manger.	T
2. Jesus was called "rabbi."	T
3. Jesus claimed to be God.	T
4. Jesus is both God and man.	T
5. Jesus was tempted.	T
6. Jesus sinned.	F
7. Jesus needed forgiveness.	F
8. Jesus offers forgiveness.	T

9.	Jesus has the power of God.	T
10.	Jesus got angry.	T
11.	Jesus lived in Egypt for a time.	T
12.	Joseph was Jesus' biological father.	F
13.	Jesus had a brother.	T
14.	Jesus turned stones into bread.	F
15.	Moses wrote about Jesus.	T
16.	Jesus prays for believers.	T
17.	Jesus loves all people.	T

No Trivial Matter

Divide the group into two teams and explain that you will be playing a trivia game. The problem is, you don't have the questions yet. Each team's assignment is to write ten questions about the life of Christ that the other team must answer. Give each team a Bible or two and paper and pencils, then allow five to ten minutes for them to write the questions. Have them put one question on each slip of paper with the answer on the back. Then have the teams take turns asking each other the questions. You can serve as the judge, timer, and scorekeeper.

After each question, give the team two minutes to discuss and decide on their answer. Then, one person should give the answer. Make sure that the questions are legitimate. Award 1,000 points for every correct answer. After determining the winner, make a few comments about the difficulty they had in finding good questions to ask, the answers, and how well they knew their Bibles (adapted from *Youth Meetings for LESSONmaker;* used by permission).

C. Intro to DVD: 2 minutes

Preview the DVD and prepare the group with questions to think about as they watch the segment. Explain what the DVD segment will cover and how it matches Dr. Lutzer's book.

Questions you want the participants to address:

1.

2.

3.

D. DVD Segment: 6 minutes

Watch the DVD segment together. Divide into small groups afterward to work through the material supplied for the small group leaders on pp. 60–61.

E. Small Group Discussion: 30 minutes

SMALL GROUP LEADER NOTES

1. Make sure your small group leaders have copies of the necessary handouts for the session.

2. Remember that the purpose of the small group discussions is to help members interact with the material on a personal level, to encourage members to share their experiences and their responses, and to study together.

SMALL GROUP LEADER HELPS

1. Small groups should be safe places to discuss and interact with the material. So . . .
    a. Don't monopolize the conversations, or allow a group member to do so.
    b. Ask open-ended questions:
        i. How might someone respond to what Dr. Lutzer said?
        ii. How might you interact with those who have read the book?
        iii. What concerns do you have based on what you have read or seen?
        iv. What Bible verses relate directly to what we are reading/hearing?

2. Prepare in advance so you have additional material or questions.

3. Incorporate material from both the book and the video segments.

4. Small groups should be a place to discuss the Bible together.

5. Small groups should be where God works in lives, so be sure to end the time in prayer, asking God to help everyone use the material to interact with peers, friends, and family.

PRELIMINARY SMALL GROUP DISCUSSION QUESTIONS

1. How can we respond to people who tell us that the New Testament is unreliable? (Answer: *We can say, "It has stood the test of time and rigorous scholarship."*)

2. What is the purpose of the Jesus Seminar? (Answer: *The group aims to change the way people think about Jesus and give a new view of Jesus, as one who appeals to modern concerns like feminism, ecology, multiculturalism, and political correctness—see pp. 103–104*)

3. Why do the Jesus Seminar scholars have such a hard time believing that Jesus is divine? (Answer: *They have a strong bias against the supernatural.*)

4. Augustine wrote, "If you believe what you like in the gospels and reject what you don't like, it's not the gospel you believe, but yourself" (p. 110). Is this statement valid in our culture as well as in Augustine's time? (Answer: *Yes. Modern people believe strongly in a religion of the self.*)

5. What are three tests that can be applied to verify the historical accuracy of the New Testament? (Answer: *The first test is biographical—do we have a good manuscript tradition? We can also examine internal and external evidence.*)

6. How is it possible that a fallible church could choose an infallible set of books for the New Testament? (Answer: *The revelation and inspiration of God make this possible.*)

FURTHER SMALL GROUP DISCUSSION QUESTIONS

1. Earlier you were given a quiz. How did you do? Are you willing to share with the group?

2. What are common misunderstandings about Jesus among your friends?

3. What are common errors in your own thinking about Jesus?

4. Did you do better than you thought you would, or worse?

5. In response to what you are hearing about *The Da Vinci Code* and all the conspiracies and fabrications, do you doubt what you know about Jesus? Why or why not?

6. On p. 102, Dr. Lutzer quotes the character, Robert Langdon, a Harvard professor, who says, "Those who truly understand their faiths understand the stories are metaphorical. . . . Religious allegory has become a part of the fabric of reality. And living in that reality helps millions of people cope and be better people." Discuss this quote together.

7. Do you agree? Why or why not?

8. What evidence is there for this sort of logic?

9. How would you counter this sort of thinking with a peer, a colleague, or a family member?

10. What is your response to the quote on p. 105 from Robert Funk, the founder of the Jesus Seminar, who said, "The Christ of creed and dogma who had been firmly in place in the Middle Ages can no longer command the assent of those who have seen the heavens through Galileo's telescope"?

11. Do your friends and relatives believe this quote or a declaration along the same line of thought?

12. What do you think is the difficulty that the author (and your friends) may have reconciling Jesus and modern-day scientific revelations?

13. Again, how would you respond to someone who shared this struggle to reconcile the two?

14. Considering the account of the early disciples, what significance does this have for the truth of Scripture and the life and history of Jesus?

F. Message: 10–12 minutes

For the message, say something like the following:

Dr. Lutzer closes this chapter with several statements about the resistance of scholars and laypeople to embracing the deity of Christ and his supernatural qualities, such as healing, forgiving, raising people from the dead, and casting out demons. People are more comfortable with a man who was a good example and who taught pithy maxims about life and living with others, but who never really got dirty. Many don't like the fact that Jesus wants to deal with the sin as well as the sinner.

Consider the woman caught in adultery. (Read aloud John 8:1–11.) Jesus wisely buffered the accusations of the leaders who brought her before him in shame and guilt. Then Jesus forgave the woman and told her to go and sin no more. But what we don't often think about is that Jesus could actually forgive her, first, because he was God and second, because his whole purpose was to redeem people to God. He came in order to die, to take the punishment for this woman's sin. She could be forgiven because Jesus was God and because he would pay for her sin on the cross.

To remove the deity of Christ, to remove the supernatural from the accounts of Jesus, is to be left with a good man, not a Savior, not a Redeemer. The danger that exists not just in the text of *The Da Vinci Code*, but also in mainstream religiosity, is to minimize the full image of Jesus that is given to us in Scripture. Modern scholars are discontent with miracles, supernatural activity, and angels and demons because to admit such things would make them culpable for the errors of their ways. To admit that Jesus is in fact God is to confess the truth of his claims and then be responsible for what he says about the need for him, the call to confession and repentance, and finally, the call to discipleship.

We should not be surprised at scholarly efforts to remove anything that might make ultimate or eternal expectations of the reader or the hearer of the Word of God. We should not be surprised that people want to remove everything but the quotes and anecdotes, good ideas and suggestions for healthy living. If this is all that is found in Scripture, then readers can reject whatever does not fit their paradigm or anything that makes them too uncomfortable. As sinful humans we don't like having to submit to the fact that someone else might know better, have a greater understanding, or have truth that would require us to change our ways.

In our sinful responses, then, we criticize, poke holes, and seek errors rather than truth. We look for failure, not in a scholarly sense of seeking accuracy and consistency, but in a way that helps us escape the truth of a gospel that demands humility and change. Our self-seeking critique puts us above Scripture, making ourselves editors—cutting, replacing, removing, or adding where we see problems or discomfort. Instead of sitting under the wisdom of Scripture that has been consistent for centuries, we feel we have come to some greater realization because we have new sources and hidden truths that call into question the most reliable sources.

Dr. Lutzer does a fine job of showing the truth and reliability of Scripture. Regardless of the bias of the reader or the scholar, the documents of the New Testament are sound, based on the testimony of the disciples and eyewitnesses, the growth of the early church, and the pervasiveness and immutability of Scripture since its first copy. We can thus approach the new criticisms found in *The Da Vinci Code*—the hidden truths, the conspiracy to hide and censor truth—with confidence and security, knowing that God is working to protect his name. He is alive and well, and his Word will not return void.

G. Personal Application/Response (optional): 15 minutes

This week, read the account of the Prodigal Son in Luke 15. This is the final parable in a series of parables about lost items: the lost sheep, the lost coin, and the lost son. If you have access to the *Life Application Bible*, review the study notes to understand what is going on in the text and why certain aspects of the story are significant.

Meditate on this passage. Spend time reading and rereading—placing yourself in the story and imagining the feelings of various characters: the father, the younger son, the older brother, a servant, a friend of the father, and so on. Then look back at the passage. Circle, underline, and memorize segments of Scripture that are poignant statements about the mercy and grace that flows from the Father.

As you read, answer these questions:

1. What did it mean that the younger son asked for his inheritance?
2. In verse 17, what does it mean when this son "came to his senses"?
3. Watch the older brother's response. What is his argument to his father?
4. With which brother do you most identify? Why? When?
5. When have you held resentment for what others have done to wrong you? Or against those who seem to have received more mercy than you?
6. Why do you think you responded that way?
7. What does the older brother's bitterness indicate?
8. In what way did the father show mercy to the younger brother?
9. Who does the father represent in this passage?
10. In what way(s) have you received mercy in lieu of punishment for your errors?
11. What truth(s) can you glean from this story about the Father?
12. How is this mercy possible for us today in the twenty-first century?
13. What is required of believers as we understand this passage?

H. Homework: 5 minutes

Encourage everyone to do a little work outside of your regular session time, following these suggestions:

1. Read through the Gospels this week; write down in a journal the images, truths, and character qualities of Jesus that strike you. Consider memorizing passages that encourage you.
2. Memorize some of the verses that Dr. Lutzer offers in the chapter that give support to the accuracy of Scripture:
    a. Isaiah 40:8
    b. John 21:24–25
    c. 2 Peter 1:16
    d. 2 Peter 1:19–21
3. Prepare for next week by reading Chapter Six: "Divergent Paths: The Church and its Competitors."
    a. Underline and mark up the book as you read.
    b. Write down any questions you have that you come across.
    c. Read through the text with your Bible at the ready, look up verses and read Scripture in response and in addition to what is in the Dr. Lutzer book.

I. Handouts and Worksheets: 5 minutes

Have several copies of the handouts to give to your group members this week:

1. Chapter Quiz
2. Chapter Summary
3. Personal Response

CHAPTER QUIZ (p. 99)

Take the following quiz to see how well you remember the details of Chapter Five:

1. What is the name of the organization that meets to discuss and vote on the validity of the sayings of Jesus? (Answer: *The Jesus Seminar*)

2. What percent of Jesus' sayings would this organization attribute to Jesus' actual sayings? (Answer: *Only about 18%*)

3. According to the Jesus Seminar, is Jesus more than a man? (Answer: *No*)

4. In the book, *The Five Gospels*, what are the five Gospels? (Answer: *Matthew, Mark, Luke, John, and Thomas*)

5. Scholars believe that in order to find the true historical Jesus, those studying the Gospels should evaluate them as any other historical work. True or False? (Answer: *True*)

6. What are the tests that John Warwick Montgomery suggests for testing the accuracy of the New Testament documents? For extra credit, give a brief statement of what each test means (pp. 111–115). (Answer: *Biographical test, internal test, external test*)

7. What is the approximate gap in years between the original and the copies of New Testament texts? (Answer: *Approximately 250 years*)

8. What is the approximate gap in years for copies of Plato's works? (Answer: *Approximately 1,300 years*)

9. Were any of the books of the New Testament written by eyewitnesses? (Answer: *Yes*)

10. What doctrinal truth about Christ would have been outrageous for any practicing Jew to believe? (Answer: *That a human being was divine.*)

CHAPTER SUMMARY (p. 100)

Dr. Lutzer opens this chapter with a short review of the Jesus Seminar, an organization that meets semiannually in California. During their meetings, members cast votes (colored beads) on whether they believe various Jesus events and teachings recorded in the Bible are historical. They have concluded that only about 18 percent of what is attributed to Jesus is actually true. And those statements and activities fit nicely into modern hot topics like feminism, ecology, and political correctness. These scholars, however, do not support the possibility of miracles and the supernatural. In fact, the founder of the Jesus Seminar stated that a person couldn't believe the New Testament version of Jesus, after having seen the cosmos through Galileo's telescope (p. 105).

Dr. Lutzer follows this introduction by emphasizing the responsibility readers and scholars have to respect the historicity of documents and to not pick and choose based on personal liking and comfort levels. To make decisions based on personal whim or comfort is to create history in the eyes of the beholder with little or no accountability to dozens or hundreds of other supporting records that validate the account. If there is no responsibility, the reader can "make sense" of the miracles and claims to lordship by saying Jesus was crazy, deluded, or fanatical, but surely not the Messiah. Dr. Lutzer states that the reader is faced with a clear choice: *Either accept Jesus as he is portrayed in the New Testament or confess ignorance about him.*

Next Dr. Lutzer develops the validity of the New Testament texts through an evaluation method that considers three aspects of the documents under consideration. The first is the *biographical test*, which asks the question, "If we do not have the original, by what means do we have the current copies, and is this tradition reliable?" The second test, the *internal test*, questions the claims of the writer of the work. The internal test determines whether the writer was an eyewitness, knew the author, was somewhat related to the work, or has no real connection to the work (a pseudopigrapha). The third test is the *external test*. This test compares the present material with other historical documents to see if other documents support the same facts, events, ideas, or people.

Dr. Lutzer addresses the eyewitness testimonies of the disciples and other followers as valid. He states with support that the disciples would not have raised these claims that Jesus was the Messiah, the Son of God. In other New Testament documents, letters to churches and individuals, we see eyewitnesses, Peter, James, and John advocating for Jesus, saying they saw these activities with their own eyes. They not only saw; they also heard and touched him following the Resurrection. These followers can confirm the prophecies that Christ fulfilled. They confirm what we read in the New Testament. They are witnesses to the activities and claims of Christ.

PERSONAL RESPONSE (p. 101)

Make copies of the "Personal Response" sheet to distribute to everyone.

J. Other Resources (optional)

Consider the following resources this week if you have time:

1. Books to consider:
    a. Strobel, Lee. *The Case for Christ*. Grand Rapids, MI: Zondervan Publishing, 1998.
    b. Strobel, Lee. *The Case for Faith*, see especially "Objection #5: It's Offensive to Claim Jesus Is the Only Way to God, p. 145." Grand Rapids, MI: Zondervan Publishing, 2000.
2. Videos/TV/Internet:
    a. *Jesus Among Other Gods* by Ravi Zacharias. This video, with an EZ Lesson Plan, is based on the popular book of the same name.
    b. Do a Web search for "The Jesus Seminar" for the Web site associated with this organization and the Westar Institute.
    c. *From Jesus to Christ*, PBS Frontline Special, first aired 1998.

SESSION SEVEN:
DIVERGENT PATHS: THE CHURCH AND ITS COMPETITORS

Introduction

LESSON TEXT
Dr. Lutzer, Chapter Six: "Divergent Paths: The Church and Its Competitors"

LESSON KEY FOCUS/IDEA
The purpose of this session is to help participants distinguish the difference between Christianity and other competing philosophies, namely Gnosticism and its derivatives. The chapter sets apart Christianity from other religions that believe in God because Christianity asserts the necessity of Jesus for salvation.

LESSON GOALS
As a result of this session, participants will:
1. See how Christianity differs from Gnosticism.
2. Learn how Christianity is unique.
3. Hear the saving Gospel of Christ.

LESSON MATERIALS
The Da Vinci Deception books, Bibles, pens, paper, handouts, small group questions, DVD

LESSON FORMAT

A. Welcome	3–5 minutes
B. Opening Activities (optional)	10–15 minutes
C. Intro to DVD	2 minutes
D. DVD Segment	6 minutes
E. Small Group Discussion:	30 minutes
F. Message	10–12 minutes
G. Personal Application/Response (optional)	15 minutes
H. Homework	5 minutes
I. Handouts and Worksheets	5 minutes
a. Chapter Quiz	
b. Chapter Summary	
c. Personal Response	
J. Other Resources (optional)	

A. Welcome: 3–5 minutes

1. Welcome everyone back, and greet new people who may have joined the group.
2. Explain to participants why you are covering *The Da Vinci Deception* (from Author's Note, p. xiii):
    a. Investigate the historical roots of Christianity.
    b. Give credible answers to questions like these:
        i. Who is Jesus?
        ii. Is the New Testament a reliable source?
        iii. What should this mean to us in the twenty-first century?
3. Review last week's material with the group—what was covered and what the group should have done to prepare for the session (see the previous lesson). They should have:
    a. Found answers for the significant questions of the Christian faith.
    b. Found encouragement in the accuracy and reliability of the Scriptures of the Old and New Testaments.
4. Present a brief overview of what the group will do at the current session. They will:
    a. See how Christianity differs from Gnosticism.
    b. Learn how Christianity is unique.
    c. Hear the saving Gospel of Christ.

B. Opening Activities (optional): 10–15 minutes

CHECKING IN

Instead of a game or get-to-know-you activity, spend some time checking in with your group. Ask the following questions to see where your group is in processing *The Da Vinci Deception*:

1. What have you learned while taking this class?
2. What opportunities have you had to engage with others about the material?
3. What has been the response of others you know who are aware that you are reading this book?

ESCAPE!

Bring a pair of handcuffs and hold them up. Explain that you want volunteers to put them on and then try to get out of them. There is a trick to it, but it is possible to escape. As an incentive, offer a prize to the first person who can escape within 30 seconds.

Bring up the first contestant, put on the handcuffs, and watch him or her work to get them off. When 30 seconds are up, unlock the cuffs, remove them, and repeat with the next person. (Note: These should be real handcuffs that can be removed only by using the key.) If none of these volunteers can figure out how to escape, bring up a staff member who knows how. Put the cuffs on him or her and say, "Go." He or she should simply say, "Will you please let me out?" That's the trick! All the person had to do was ask. Unlock the handcuffs and release him or her.

Afterward, ask how this is an illustration of how we are saved. Trapped in our sins, we can try all sorts of ways to extricate ourselves. But the truth is that only Christ holds the key. He is ready and willing to let us out; all we have to do is ask. (From *Youth Meetings for LESSONmaker*, used by permission.)

C. Intro to DVD: 2 minutes

Preview the DVD and prepare the group with questions to think about as they watch the segment. Explain what the DVD segment will cover and how it matches Dr. Lutzer's book.

Questions you want the participants to address:

1.

2.

3.

D. DVD Segment: 6 minutes

Watch the DVD segment together. Divide into small groups afterward to work through the material supplied for the small group leaders on pp. 69–70.

E. Small Group Discussion: 30 minutes

SMALL GROUP LEADER NOTES:

1. Make sure your small group leaders have copies of the necessary handouts for the session.
2. Remember that the purpose of the small group discussions is to help members interact with the material on a personal level, to encourage members to share their experiences and their responses, and to study together.

SMALL GROUP LEADER HELPS:

1. Small groups should be safe places to discuss and interact with the material. So . . .
    a. Don't monopolize the conversations or allow a group member to do so.
    b. Ask open-ended questions:
        i. How might someone respond to what Dr. Lutzer said?
        ii. How might you interact with those who have read the book?
        iii. What concerns do you have based on what you have read or seen?
        iv. What Bible verses relate directly to what we are reading/hearing?
2. Prepare in advance so you have additional material or questions.
3. Incorporate material from both the book and video segments.

4. Small groups should be places to discuss the Bible together.

5. Small groups should be where God works in lives, so be sure to end the time in prayer, asking God to help everyone use the material to interact with peers, friends, and family.

PRELIMINARY SMALL GROUP DISCUSSION QUESTIONS:

1. What can we say to someone who thinks that all religions are the same? (Answer: *We can reply, "Christianity is different from other religions in many respects. All religions cannot be correct, because they contradict each other."*)

2. Why is our culture so attracted to Gnosticism and its teaching? (Answer: *Many people want to connect with the metaphysical world, yet they are committed to diversity and cafeteria-style religion where they can pick and choose what to believe. Gnosticism also appeals because according to this philosophy, no one religion is "right"—they are all valid, and personal salvation is in the hands of the individual rather than God.*)

3. In what ways do Christian beliefs differ from other religions? (Answer: *Christianity acknowledges the doctrine of sin, the inability to redeem ourselves, the holiness of God, and the reality of a Redeemer who can rescue us.*)

4. What can we say to someone who says, "I'm into God, but not Jesus"? (Answer: *We can say, "The Bible says we are not to make remake God according to our own liking [see p. 142]. Jesus is the only way to God."*)

5. What advice would you have for someone who is considering reading *The Da Vinci Code*? How would you respond to the statement, "It's only fiction"?

FURTHER SMALL GROUP DISCUSSION QUESTIONS

1. How would you walk someone through the gospel who has questions about the nature and work of God in the world but has not been willing to make a commitment to Christ?

2. Why do you think people are so resistant to the gospel?

3. What kind of job does your church do in communicating the gospel to its members?

4. In what ways have you communicated the truth of the gospel this past week? What are some other options for how you can engage the gospel in your everyday life?

5. If you have a story, relay a discussion you have had with someone about the relativity of religions in the world and their understanding of Jesus.

F. Message: 10–12 minutes

For the message, say something like the following:

After reading *The Da Vinci Code* and then *The Da Vinci Deception*, your mind may be in great turmoil, thinking, processing, evaluating, and assimilating all the information. A person can get really lost in all the research and the supporting documents. We may find ourselves confused or angry because we

cannot grasp all the facts, all the defenses that each book sets forth. Questions and qualifications may be swimming in our minds: What about this? What about that? Where was that fact—I can't remember? We may be disheartened or fearful when we consider sharing this information with our friends because we are afraid we will forget an important point or that we will make a mistake.

Those fears are natural. But they are also sinful. They are sinful because they neglect the work of the Holy Spirit in the lives of people. These fears are in a sense prideful because they put human work and abilities over and above the abilities of the Spirit to convict. They are prideful because they forget the promises found in Scripture, that salvation is a gift of God to be received through faith (Ephesians 2:8–9)— not from fancy words or well-oiled arguments. A person's salvation rests in the work of God, and we are called to participate in the work God is doing in the world. Our responsibility, then, as believers, is to respond to the inklings in our hearts, the subtle thoughts that run through our minds, to share the Good News of the Gospel of Christ. When we respond, we are creating opportunities for further discussion with those around us who have fallen into this works-oriented, sinless heresy called Gnosticism.

Let's read this passage aloud. John 15:9–16:16:

9 "I have loved you even as the Father has loved me. Remain in my love. 10 When you obey my commandments, you remain in my love, just as I obey my Father's commandments and remain in his love. 11 I have told you these things so that you will be filled with my joy. Yes, your joy will overflow! 12 This is my commandment: Love each other in the same way I have loved you. 13 There is no greater love than to lay down one's life for one's friends. 14 You are my friends if you do what I command. 15 I no longer call you slaves, because a master doesn't confide in his slaves. Now you are my friends, since I have told you everything the Father told me. 16 You didn't choose me. I chose you. I appointed you to go and produce lasting fruit, so that the Father will give you whatever you ask for, using my name. 17 This is my command: Love each other.

18 "If the world hates you, remember that it hated me first. 19 The world would love you as one of its own if you belonged to it, but you are no longer part of the world. I chose you to come out of the world, so it hates you. 20 Do you remember what I told you? 'A slave is not greater than the master.' Since they persecuted me, naturally they will persecute you. And if they had listened to me, they would listen to you 21 They will do all this to you because of me, for they have rejected the One who sent me. 22 They would not be guilty if I had not come and spoken to them. But now they have no excuse for their sin. 23 Anyone who hates me also hates my Father. 24 If I hadn't done such miraculous signs among them that no one else could do, they would not be guilty. But as it is, they have seen everything I did, yet they still hate me and my Father. 25 This fulfills what is written in their Scriptures: 'They hated me without cause.'

26 "But I will send you the Advocate —the Spirit of truth. He will come to you from the Father and will testify all about me. 27 And you must also testify about me because you have been with me from the beginning of my ministry.

6:1 "I have told you these things so that you won't abandon your faith. 2 For you will be expelled from the synagogues, and the time is coming when those who kill you will think they are doing a holy service for God. 3 This is because they have never known the Father or me. 4 Yes, I'm telling you these things now, so that when they happen, you will remember my warning. I didn't tell you earlier because I was going to be with you for a while longer.

⁵ "But now I am going away to the One who sent me, and not one of you is asking where I am going. ⁶ Instead, you grieve because of what I've told you. ⁷ But in fact, it is best for you that I go away, because if I don't, the Advocate won't come. If I do go away, then I will send him to you. ⁸ And when he comes, he will convict the world of its sin, and of God's righteousness, and of the coming judgment. ⁹ The world's sin is that it refuses to believe in me. ¹⁰ Righteousness is available because I go to the Father, and you will see me no more. ¹¹ Judgment will come because the ruler of this world has already been judged.

¹² "There is so much more I want to tell you, but you can't bear it now. ¹³ When the Spirit of truth comes, he will guide you into all truth. He will not speak on his own but will tell you what he has heard. He will tell you about the future. ¹⁴ He will bring me glory by telling you whatever he receives from me. ¹⁵ All that belongs to the Father is mine; this is why I said, 'The Spirit will tell you whatever he receives from me.' ¹⁶ "In a little while you won't see me anymore. But a little while after that, you will see me again."

Jesus knew that persecution and resistance would await the disciples. He knew they had many questions that would have to remain unanswered, and they would have many after he was gone. The promise of the Spirit to the disciples is also an encouragement to believers today.

Here's the truth: God loves us; we are cherished. God does not want to leave us to our own wisdom and subsequent failure; he does not want us to be confused or disheartened. So God has promised the Spirit to come and minister to us. The Holy Spirit is the Revealer, the Comforter, and the Pray-er (Romans 8). God the Father has thought all this through. God the Son has told us this plainly. God the Spirit fills this void, reveals truth, convicts of sin, and reminds us that we are the children of God. Let us give thanks and pray with confidence. Let us speak the truth in love. Let us go forth in confidence in the faith that we profess.

Close in prayer with the group.

G. Personal Application/Response (optional): 15 minutes

In the space below, write out, or if you have a recorder, tape yourself sharing the gospel, the story of sinful men and women redeemed and forgiven through the work of Jesus Christ on the cross. Afterward, listen to yourself and write down the main points.

1. What did you forget to mention?

Go back to Scripture and find passages that communicate the gospel and a sinner's need for salvation. What in the story of the gospel really resonates with you? Why?

1. Your sin?
2. God's love?
3. God's grace?
4. Christ's suffering?

Pray for an opportunity this week to share this message with someone you know: a family member, friend, or colleague.

H. Homework: 5 minutes

Encourage everyone to do a little extra work with these suggestions:

1. Find several Web sites of reputable Christian colleges, churches, or Christian organizations that have posted a belief statement or Statement of Faith. Print out and compare the lists, highlighting the repeated doctrinal statements.
   a. What features do the lists have in common?
   b. What elements are dissimilar?
2. Consider memorizing some of the verses that Dr. Lutzer offers in the chapter that support the accuracy of Scripture.
3. Go back and read through Matthew, Mark, Luke, and John. Consider Romans as well.
   a. Underline and mark up the Bible as you read.
   b. Write down any questions you have as you come across the material.
   c. Read through the text and look up cross-references. Use other books and resources that may help you understand the text.
4. Discuss the book you have read and what you have learned from these sessions with a friend, colleague, or family member.

I. Handouts and Worksheets: 5 minutes

Have several copies of the handouts to distribute to participants.

1. Chapter Quiz
2. Chapter Summary Sheet
3. Personal Response

CHAPTER QUIZ (p. 102)

Take the following quiz to see how well you remember the details of Chapter Six.

1. Some have said Jesus stole the identity and history of what pagan god? (Answer: *Mithras*)
2. Name one of two books Dr. Lutzer mentions where a reader can find prophecy about Jesus. (Answer: *Isaiah, Psalms*)
3. Do Gnostics believe in the necessity of the death and resurrection of Jesus? (Answer: *No*)
4. Gnostics use the word *logo* as a term that means what? (Answer: *Reason or special knowledge*)
5. In what Gnostic book is the resurrection of Christ referred to as a vision, dream, or trance? (Answer: *The Gospel of Mary*)
6. According to Gnosticism, the person's spiritual problem is _____, not _____. (Answer: *ignorance/sin*)

7. The doctrine that all men and women are born into a state of sin is called what? (Answer: *Doctrine of Original Sin*)

8. True or False: Jesus could have saved people without being either human or divine. (Answer: *False*)

9. True or False: Muslims believe that Jesus was God incarnate. (Answer: *False*)

CHAPTER SUMMARY (p. 103)

In the first half of the chapter, Dr. Lutzer lays out what Christianity is not. In the first few paragraphs, he alludes to scholars who have reduced Christianity to a list of stolen mythological facts from the legend of Mithras, popular in ancient Rome. Mithras is understood to be a god of the ancient Persians and was known as the "son of God, the Light of the world." Supposedly, he was born on December 25, died, was buried in a rock tomb, and rose from the dead three days later. However, as Dr. Lutzer states, Jesus was prophesied in the Old Testament seven centuries before Christ; those prophecies were fulfilled in the life and work of Christ. Gnosticism is a perversion and a tangent from the true gospel of Christ. It appeals to people today, to their desire to connect with the metaphysical world. A Gnostic teaching will allow the adherent to essentially choose his or her own path, selecting what he or she likes and dislikes.

In order to deal with people's need for salvation, the Jesus captured in the Gospel narrative must be real; he must be true. The acts of healing, the forgiving of sins, the raising of dead people, the teachings, and the fulfilling of prophecy must be real, not imaginary. To name them as mirages is to remove the ability of Jesus to be Savior, who mediates for believers at the right hand of God the Father. In removing Christ's divinity and making his death a ruse, Gnostics believe that we encounter God in ourselves, in our divine inner spark of enlightenment, our "gnosis." Flying in the face of Scripture that tells of our sinful state, Gnosticism says we are not sinful, just ignorant.

Gnosticism is not another viable version of Christianity. In addition, we cannot mix and match what we like best from the world's religions, or claim they are all equal options.

How is Christianity different than what we see in other religions? First, we find the doctrine of sin—the truth that all people, in all times and all places, are affected by original sin. Everyone is born with a sin nature that causes actual sins, which we commit and which are committed against us. Second, everyone is held to a perfect law from a perfect God. In order to be in the presence of God, we must be perfect. Third, Jesus comes on the scene as the God-man, fully God and fully human, able to bridge the divide and meet the demands of the penalty of sin: death. The Incarnate Word, the Savior, Jesus is the connection between God and people, and he is the only possible connection. We cannot earn salvation; we cannot achieve it on our own, as Gnosticism and other religions profess.

We cannot change God into our own liking; we cannot make him as we wish; we cannot approach him through any means other than faith in the saving work of Jesus Christ. This is the Good News—the faith we profess in Jesus Christ. To put our hope in our own works and efforts to be enlightened is *bad news* for sure.

PERSONAL RESPONSE (p. 104)

Make copies of the "Personal Response" to hand out to your participants.

J. Other Resources (optional)

Consider the following resources this week if you have time.

1. Books:

    a. Yamauchi, Edwin M. *Pre-Christian Gnosticis*. Grand Rapids, MI: Eerdmans, 1973.

    b. Lutzer, Erwin. *Christ Among Other Gods*. Chicago, IL: Moody Publishing, 1997.

    c. McDowell, Josh. *Handbook of Today's Religions*. Nashville, TN: Thomas Nelson Publishers, 1992.

    d. Martin, Walter. *Kingdom of the Cults*. Minneapolis, MN: Bethany House Publishers, rev. 2003.

Botticelli—An Italian painter from Florence who was extremely successful at the peak of his career, with a highly individual and graceful style founded on the rhythmic capabilities of outline; one of the best-loved quattrocento painters through the interest of Ruskin and the Pre-Raphaelites.

Christology—Christology is that part of theology which deals with Jesus Christ. In its full extent it comprises the doctrines concerning both the person of Christ and his works.

Constantine—Born at Naissus, now Nisch in Servia [Nis, Serbia —*Ed.*], he was the son of a Roman officer, Constantius, and became the Roman Emperor. The date of his birth is not certain, being given as early as 274 and as late as 288.

Council of Nicaea—First Ecumenical Council of the Catholic Church, held in AD 325 on the occasion of the heresy of Arius.

Deity of Christ—The Christian doctrine that states Jesus of Nazareth was in fact God incarnate and that he retained the nature of God while present on earth.

The Gnostic Bible—A collection of Gnostic writings which includes such books as the Gospel of Philip, the Gospel of Mary, the Gospel of Thomas, and other cryptic, esoteric quotes and descriptions of Jesus. Gnostic thought claims that people are saved through enlightenment; people are not sinful.

Gnosticism—A pre-Christian and early Christian religious movement teaching that salvation comes by learning esoteric spiritual truths that free humanity from the material world, believed in this movement to be evil.

Grace—The infinite love, mercy, favor, and goodwill shown to humankind by God. Its greatest manifestation is the gift of the Son for salvation.

Heresy—An opinion or belief that contradicts established religious teaching, especially one that is officially condemned by a religious authority.

Holy Grail—According to medieval legend, the cup said to be used by Jesus Christ at the Last Supper and by Joseph of Arimathea to collect his blood and sweat at the Crucifixion. According to *The Da Vinci Code*, the "grail" was Mary Magdalene, and the cup was never present at the Lord's Supper (the way Leonardo da Vinci pictured it)—a secret that the Roman Catholic Church wants no one to know.

Jesus Seminar—A group of modern scholars who meet semiannually to discuss the accuracy of quotes or actions attributed to Jesus as recorded in the Bible. These scholars vote with small colored beads on whether or not a particular quote should or should not be attributed to Jesus.

Knights Templar—One of the three major orders of medieval Christian knights active in Palestine during the Crusades, according to *The Da Vinci Code*. The military order of the Priory of Sion is supposed to have included members such as Isaac Newton and Victor Hugo, in addition to Leonardo da Vinci.

Last Supper—The last meal that Jesus Christ ate with his disciples before his crucifixion, commemorated by Christians in the Communion ceremony. This meal is portrayed in the painting of the same name by Leonardo da Vinci that Brown claims hides secrets about the truth about Jesus.

Leonardo da Vinci—(1452–1519), A Florentine artist; one of the great masters of the High Renaissance; celebrated as a painter, sculptor, architect, etc.; at the center of the book *The Da Vinci Code*; alleged member of the Priory of Sion.

Louvre Museum—The national art museum of France and the palace in which it is housed, located in Paris on the right bank of the Seine River.

Erwin W. Lutzer—Senior pastor of The Moody Church since 1980; was born and reared near Regina, Saskatchewan, Canada. He is an award-winning author of more than twenty books and a celebrated international conference speaker.

Mary Magdalene—Woman so named from Magdala, a town near Tiberias (now in Israel) whom Jesus healed of evil spirits. In *The Da Vinci Code* she is said to be married to Jesus and is the mother of their daughter.

The Masons—A secret or esoteric worldwide fraternal organization. Its members are reportedly joined together by shared ideals of both morality and metaphysics. Most branches have a constitutional declaration of belief in a Supreme Being.

Merovingians—Dynasty of kings that ruled the Franks, a Germanic tribe, from AD 481 to 751.

New Testament—The second section of the Christian Bible dealing with the life and teachings of Jesus Christ and containing the Gospels, the Acts of the Apostles, the Epistles, and the book of Revelation.

Nicene Creed—A formal statement of Christian beliefs formulated at the first Nicene Council, held in Nicaea in AD 325, subsequently altered and expanded and still in use in most Christian churches.

Opus Dei—The supposed secret organization of the Roman Catholic Church commissioned with keeping secret the truths that the Priory of Sion holds. According to *The Da Vinci Code*, this secret organization will use whatever means necessary to keep quiet those who know the truth about Jesus, Mary, the Holy Grail, and much more, things the Catholic Church doesn't want anyone to know.

Orthodoxy—Relating to following the established or traditional rules of social behavior, a philosophy, or a faith.

Postmodernism—Any of a wide-ranging set of developments in critical theory, philosophy, architecture, art, literature, history, and culture, which are generally characterized as either emerging from, in reaction to, or superseding modernism. Postmodernism generally questions truth and the ability to know truth.

Priory of Sion—A priory is a religious community or home, such as a monastery or convent, headed by a prior or prioress. According to *The Da Vinci Code*, this priory claims that Jesus and Mary were married and had a child and that the Catholic Church conspired to keep Mary Magdalene from assuming the foundation of the church, instead passing that honor to Peter. Supposedly, members of the Priory of Sion hid these "facts" in paintings, music, and other forms of art.

Renaissance—The period in European history from about the fourteenth through sixteenth centuries regarded as marking the end of the Middle Ages and featuring major cultural and artistic change; also, the cultural and religious spirit that characterized the Renaissance, including the decline of Gothic architecture, the revival of classical culture, the beginnings of modern science, and geographical exploration.

Salvation—The Christian doctrine that states deliverance from sin and the consequences of sin (death) is through faith in the work of Jesus Christ's death on the cross.

Tarot cards—A system of fortune-telling using a special pack of 78 cards that consists of four suits of 14 cards together with 22 picture cards.

Troubadours—Lyric poets or poet-musicians of France in the eleventh to thirteenth centuries. Poets working in the south of France, writing in Provencal (*langue d'oc*), are generally termed troubadours; those of the north, writing in French (*langue d'oil*), are called trouvères.

The Vatican—The palace in the Vatican City that is used as the official residence of the pope and the administrative center of the papacy.

REPRODUCIBLE SHEETS

AUTHOR'S NOTE / PREFACE

Quiz

1. What claims are made in Dan Brown's book *The Da Vinci Code*?

2. With what family line has Brown proposed that Jesus is connected?

3. What purpose does Opus Dei play in the book?

4. What was the responsibility of the Knights Templar? Who were its supposed members?

5. According to Brown and his research, who should have succeeded Jesus in leading Christianity?

6. Why did this not happen?

7. What is the Shekinah?

8. According to one of the characters in the book, the New Testament is the result of what?

Chapter Summary

The Da Vinci Code proposes the following truths that readers may never have heard because of the supposed Catholic Church's suppression of these shattering truths:

1. Jesus and Mary Magdalene were married.
2. They had a daughter, Sarah, who married into the French royalty, the Merovingians.
3. This daughter may have had children and this lineage of Christ may still be alive even today.

In addition, the Catholic Church has been killing people to keep these and other secrets safe. An organization, Opus Dei, has been charged with protecting the truth about the life of Christ and Mary. Ancient codes and hidden truths have been implanted into paintings, music, and sculpture for centuries by the Priory of Sion and its military branch, the Knights Templar, which included members such as Victor Hugo, Isaac Newton, Mozart, and Leonardo da Vinci.

Jesus had intended for Mary Magdalene to continue the leadership of the church after he was crucified. Peter and other men did not like this, so they portrayed her as a prostitute to defame her and keep her from leadership. So the church is really the establishment of male chauvinists who are power hungry.

The "truth" is found in Old Testament verses that tell us there is a female counterpart to the male representation of God, called the Shekinah. The church hated this goddess worship and enabling of women and so doctored the Scriptures to eliminate this aspect and hence oppress women. In order to be fully enlightened as a Christian, these sources say, one must engage in sexual rituals which allow men and women to truly experience God. Of course the church hated sex, so they made it out to be a "disgusting and sinful act."

Brown goes on to claim that these secrets can be known to anyone, they are not really secrets. His research netted academia's finest who were ready and willing to talk about the truth of Christ as known in the Gnostic Gospels.

Dr. Lutzer finishes the introductory material with a call to research of his own, to study the veracity of the Scripture and to find the truth, dispelling lore and fabrications, and call readers to a right view of the Jesus as found in the New Testament.

The Gospels of John and Mark

Read the Gospel of Mark and/or the Gospel of John before the next session to get to know the Jesus of the New Testament. If you have read enough about the Jesus as known to the Gnostics, or Brown's Jesus, compare that with what you are reading in the Gospel of Mark or John.

1. What sorts of acts did Jesus perform as recorded in the New Testament?

2. How did Jesus interact with the women who were around him in ministry?

3. What is your perception of his view of women?

4. What was Jesus' view of himself?

5. What view of Jesus did the disciples have?

6. What claims did Jesus make in the text you are reading?

7. What questions are raised for you that you could ask someone who knows Scripture well?

Personal Response

In your personal study or quiet time, think through the following questions:

1. Consider the quote from Dr. Lutzer's book, "There's black Jesus, and white Jesus. Homely and handsome, capitalist and socialist, stern and hippie. Hardworking social reformer, mystical comforter" (Justin Pope).

    a. How have I created Jesus in my own eyes?

    b. How have I restricted Jesus to be what I want?

2. Does *The Da Vinci Code* cause me to doubt?
    a. How? Why?
    b. How do I respond to this doubt?

3. Looking honestly at my personal study, am I familiar enough with Scripture to interact well with a book like *The Da Vinci Code*? Where am I strong? Where am I lacking?

CHRISTIANITY, A POLITICIAN, AND A CREED

Quiz

1. According to *The Da Vinci Code*, what happened at the Council of Nicaea?

2. According to Brown's book, why did Constantine call the meeting?

3. When did the Council of Nicaea meet?

4. In what modern country is Nicaea?

5. In actuality, the Council of Nicaea was convened to refute whom? Why?

6. What are the implications of this early theologian's views?

7. Who are three of the four theologians that Dr. Lutzer names who embraced the deity of Christ before the council ever met?

8. List at least two passages in the New Testament that declare the divinity of Christ.

9. What Roman structure was mentioned in the chapter? What was its significance?

10. What heresy is alluded to in the first chapter? What are some of its claims?

Chapter Summary

The chapter opens with the account of Constantine, who, in his desire to overthrow Rome, had a vision of the cross of Christ and was told in the vision to conquer under the banner of the cross. He did so, overthrowing, conquering, and eventually establishing the Edict of Milan, which offered freedom of religion for Christians. In addition, knowing the passion that theologians had for right doctrine, he issued a decree that the bishops meet to clarify what Scripture says about Christ and his deity. Arius had been promoting a doctrine that stripped Jesus of his deity, making him more than a man but not God. The ecumenical council met in Nicaea to establish the doctrine of Christ. Arius was declared a heretic, and the doctrine was secured by the bishops, using the Greek term *homoousius* to communicate the deity of Christ. *The Da Vinci Code* is wrong in asserting that Constantine fabricated the deity of Christ to give him more power.

Dr. Lutzer continues to develop the argument that Jesus' deity was secure before the ecumenical council, and that meeting was simply a formality to halt more arguing among orthodox Christians. Dr. Lutzer calls the witness of the church fathers including Polycarp, Justin Martyr, Irenaeus, and Tertullian who embraced the deity of Christ long before the council met. Dr. Lutzer continues by showing support from the early church, the martyrs who were killed for declaring the lordship and deity of Christ under pain of death. They were required once a year to submit homage to Caesar as lord, as a god. Martyrs did not submit to this authority, so they were in effect declaring the lordship and deity of Christ.

The Da Vinci Code also claims that the council meeting at Nicaea was an act to codify the canon of the New Testament, compiling books that raised men above women, securing the power of the male-dominated church, to hide the truth about Jesus' marriage to Mary, and to secure their stance of sexual repression. This stands in opposition to the "truths" expressed in the Gnostic Gospels that raise up the divine feminine, sexual purification rites, and propose that Jesus and Mary were married and had a child.

Here are a few implications from the chapter:

1. The testimony of the council was that the deity had already been agreed upon before the meeting, not determined at the meeting.
2. Other major church fathers had already embraced the deity of Christ.
3. Early Christians were willing to die or be persecuted for the deity of Christ because they knew the truth.
4. The deity of Christ is essential for the salvation of men and women.
5. The Gnostic heresy has existed throughout history and still exists today in books like *The Da Vinci Code* and the Gnostic Bible.

Personal Response

1. Review the Nicene Creed and meditate on the descriptions in the texts. Is this the faith that you profess?

2. Spend time looking up verses for each of the tenets set forth in the Creed:

   The Nicene Creed
   I believe in one God, the Father Almighty, Maker of heaven and earth, and of all things visible and invisible.

   And in one Lord Jesus Christ, the only-begotten Son of God, begotten of the Father before all worlds; God of God, Light of Light, very God of very God; begotten, not made, being of one substance with the Father, by whom all things were made.

   Who, for us men for our salvation, came down from heaven, and was incarnate by the Holy Spirit of the virgin Mary, and was made man; and was crucified also for us under Pontius Pilate; He suffered and was buried; and the third day He rose again, according to the Scriptures; and ascended into heaven, and sits on the right hand of the Father; and He shall come again, with glory, to judge the quick and the dead; whose kingdom shall have no end.

   And I believe in the Holy Ghost, the Lord and Giver of Life; who proceeds from the Father and the Son; who with the Father and the Son together is worshipped and glorified; who spoke by the prophets.

   And I believe one holy catholic and apostolic Church. I acknowledge one baptism for the remission of sins; and I look for the resurrection of the dead, and the life of the world to come. Amen.

3. In your circle of friends, with what in this creed would they have difficulty? Why?

4. Spend time in prayer for your family and friends who may be confused about the real Jesus, or who may have difficulty accepting the truths set forth in Scripture.

THAT OTHER BIBLE

Quiz

1. Which of the following is *not* in the Gnostic Bible:
   a. The Gospel of Mary
   b. The Gospel of Philip
   c. The Gospel of Thomas
   d. The Gospel of Mark

2. In what Gnostic Gospel is the reference to the marriage of Jesus and Mary Magdalene?

3. *Gnostic* comes from what Greek word? Meaning what?

4. When and where were the Gnostic Gospels found?

5. In what language were the Gnostic Gospels written?

6. What does "spurious authorship" mean?

7. The Apocrypha is part of the Gnostic Bible—True or False.

8. In *The Da Vinci Deception*, whose account is shown to be a reliable witness to the life of Jesus?

Chapter Summary

This chapter is Dr. Lutzer's response to the Gnostic Gospels, which are addressed frequently in Brown's book *The Da Vinci Code*, as being a more accurate and complete representation of the historical Jesus. Dr. Lutzer responds to the assertion that these new "gospels" are more reliable with an argument that includes late dates, spurious authorships, and the revelation of the cryptic, nonsensical teachings included in the books.

Dr. Lutzer opens the chapter with a quick overview of the definition of Gnosticism (from the Greek word *gnosis*: meaning "knowledge"), and the philosophical roots in Platonic thought and ideas that matter is evil. This implies that God would never have become human because to do so, he would become evil.

In the meat of the chapter, Dr. Lutzer recounts the history of the documents, most importantly their late dates—removed from the life of Christ by nearly twice the amount of time as the New Testament Gospels. Also included in this recounting is the spurious authorship where authors of the Gnostic texts would attach known apostles to the letters to give them credibility. Finally, Dr. Lutzer draws our attention to the conflicting and obscure ideas presented in the teachings of the Gnostic Gospels, giving examples for the reader to view.

In the last half of the chapter, Dr. Lutzer develops the idea that sometimes history can be written to bolster psychological or political ideals. Dr. Lutzer cites other historians, Raymond Brown (no relation to Dan Brown) and Andrew Greeley, who disagree with the accuracy, validity, and helpfulness of the Gnostic Gospels. In contrast, Dr. Lutzer shows us the historian and doctor Luke of the New Testament who undertook the effort to compile an historical record for Theophilus.

Dr. Lutzer closes the chapter with a call to response from the reader. Declaring that we have a choice to accept the teachings of the New Testament or the convoluted teachings of self-seeking Gnostic spirituality, Dr. Lutzer bids the reader to choose the narrow gate, the way that clearly and ultimately separates Christianity from Gnosticism as the only path to salvation.

Personal Response

1. Spend time in silent meditation on this material, allowing space and quiet to hear the voice of God.

    a. In what ways have you limited the scope of Jesus' claims to lordship, divinity, humanity?

    b. In what ways have you allowed the buzz of life instead of Scripture to construct your thinking?

    c. Do you have doubts about the claims that Christ has made or the account of those claims as expressed in the Old and New Testaments?

    d. Are your friends Christians? Or do they tend toward Gnostic thought, saying that there are multiple ways to God?

    e. How do you respond to this?

    f. How have you talked with them about this issue?

    g. How would you talk with them about this issue?

2. Read pp. 48–50 in Dr. Lutzer's book.

    a. What is your response to the Elaine Pagel's quote from the *Time Magazine* article? How does it "sit with you"?

    b. How might you respond to someone who shared this thought with you personally?

3. Pray for those who are deceived by false teaching and are caught in the rush of twenty-first century spirituality. Pray that the Holy Spirit will move in their lives and reveal their error and confusion, allowing them to see the true Christ in Scripture.

4. Consider memorizing the passages that you discussed in your small group.

JESUS, MARY MAGDALENE, AND THE SEARCH FOR THE HOLY GRAIL

Quiz

1. In Mary's name, to what does Magdalene refer?

2. What relationship does Mary have with Jesus according to New Testament Scriptures?

3. Who is named as responsible for slandering the name of Mary Magdalene?

4. What was the name of the organization that was charged with protecting the information about the marriage between Jesus and Mary?

5. What Catholic organization directly opposed the above mentioned group?

6. According to the art historians mentioned in Dr. Lutzer's book, what is their response to *The Da Vinci Code*'s view of *The Last Supper*?

7. Why was the Holy Grail so great a treasure for people to seek?

8. What is the *Sang Real*?

9. Referring to pp. 65–66 of Dr. Lutzer's book, what is the failure of the translation of the Gospel of Philip?

10. Does Dr. Lutzer believe the account of Philip is credible? Why or why not?

11. Could Jesus have been married? Why or why not?

Chapter Summary

This chapter responds to the assertion in *The Da Vinci Code* that Jesus and Mary were, in fact, married and had a love child, perhaps with lineage extending to the present through French Royalty. It also responds to the view that Leonardo da Vinci painted *The Last Supper* with hidden secret images to communicate the truth about Jesus' relationship with Mary; that, in fact, she is the "Holy Grail," bearing the child of their love.

History tells us that Leonardo was born in the fifteenth century, painted under the masters, and felt the greatest calling was to paint. The church and images in Scripture inspired his paintings, even though history indicates that he had no true interest in the spiritual truths found in the Word. According to *The Da Vinci Code*, however, Leonardo was a passionate member of the Priory of Sion, an organization entrusted with keeping the truth about the marriage and child of Jesus and Mary hidden.

Dr. Lutzer then clarifies the Mary Magdalene as found in Scripture. The New Testament tells of seven "Marys." Dr. Lutzer corrects the view that Mary Magdalene was a prostitute, a view promulgated by Pope Gregory in the sixth century. We cannot know if she was a prostitute, and to assert it is to gossip and slander another believer in Christ. As Dr. Lutzer develops our understanding of Mary Magdalene, he also addresses the Gnostic view that Jesus had an intimate, if not sexual relationship with Mary, based on a single sketchy source—the Gospel of Philip.

The Da Vinci Deception reveals some of the teachings in the Gnostic Gospels about women in the church—that they should be preachers, that Jesus wanted to found the church on Mary, that Mary was anointed using a sex ritual. As Dr. Lutzer responds, believers should be confident that such a depiction of Jesus is completely false based on his other teachings about sexual purity in the body and the mind. We can see from Scripture that the way to connect with God is not through sexual rituals but through believing in the Lord Jesus Christ (Romans 10:9).

Closing the chapter, Dr. Lutzer addresses the possibility of Jesus' marriage. Could he have been married? Is it wrong to be married? From what we can see in the Bible, nothing is wrong with marriage. Paul celebrated marriage. Thus, if Jesus had, in fact, been married, would not Paul also have included a statement to that effect—saying that Jesus was married? Scripture *does* state that Jesus *will* be married. Throughout the New Testament, Jesus is called the "Bridegroom" and believers, who make up the church, are called his "bride." Christ has saved himself for us; he has made us his own. He has loved us, and he is our marriage partner for eternity.

Personal Response

Sometime this week, skim the Gospels to review the interactions that Jesus had with women in first-century Palestine. As you scan the Scriptures, watching how Jesus spoke, healed, and welcomed these women, ask these questions:

1. How did Jesus reach the marginalized people of his day?

2. How did Jesus respond to the customs of his day? Why did he respond this way?

3. What encouragement can you find in seeing Jesus' responses?

4. How might Jesus' example apply to your relationships today?
    a. Are you marginalized? Are you being pushed aside?

    b. Are you turning your head from those around you who are not high class, beautiful, or rich?

5. What truths about Christ, about humanity, and about relationships can you see in the passages you have read?

6. What do you know to be certain about the sinful nature and the need for a holy Redeemer?

BANNED FROM THE BIBLE: WHY?

Quiz

1. What does the word *canon* mean?

2. Give three passages of Scripture that speak to the words in the Bible coming from God.

3. What five books are included in the canon that "almost did not make it"?

4. According to Dr. Lutzer, we can be certain that the canon of the Old Testament was finalized when?

5. In what city was the canon of the Old Testament agreed upon?

6. When Paul refers to Scripture, what is he referring to?

7. What is the teaching of the apostles that was not included in the canon of the New Testament?

8. What were the criteria for acceptance into the New Testament canon?

9. What happened at the Council of Hippo in AD 393?

10. According to Dr. Lutzer, what is the problem with many Gnostic writings?

Chapter Summary

Dr. Lutzer's purpose in this chapter is to distinguish the books included in the New Testament canon from those not included and the reason(s) why and when these decisions were made and who, in fact, made these decisions. According to *The Da Vinci Code*, men who wanted to change the church into a patriarchal community put the New Testament together as an act of censorship. In the first few pages of the chapter, Dr. Lutzer gives the reader a quick overview of the rejected texts and excerpts from those texts. He also alludes to the program on the History Channel, *Banned from the Bible*, which is available on DVD.

Dr. Lutzer begins his argument for the canonicity of our Bible with the Old Testament, the Hebrew Scriptures. He gives several supporting texts of God's authorizing the texts that were being used in Jewish worship, including Exodus, Deuteronomy, Joshua, 1 Samuel, and Nehemiah. He clarifies that not all works circulating at the time were considered inspired. On pp. 85–86, Dr. Lutzer states that the list of canonical Old Testament books was agreed upon by 400 BC and ratified at the Council of Jamnia in AD 90. These texts have been supported and alluded to by several New Testament figures including Paul, Luke, and Jesus himself.

The authority of the New Testament canon is also found in the authority of the character of God, not of human beings and committees. In the next section, Dr. Lutzer works through the development of the New Testament—to whom letters were written, how they were distributed, and how widely they were accepted and used. After the heretic Marcion began promoting his own list of "accepted" works, which opposed Jewish and biblical law, scholars in the early church formed their own list of authoritative books. This list is supported by other documents and the acceptance by the early church in its wide use of these texts. Ultimately these texts were affirmed by the Holy Spirit, as the church and its members were guided and they recognized the works that rightly communicate God's message to the people he loves.

Closing this chapter, Dr. Lutzer shows that the church was guided along in its selection of canonical Scriptures in the same way that each individual writer was led by the Spirit in the writing of the letters, narrative, law, or poetry. In the way that we accept the infallible writings of fallible men led by the Spirit, we also accept the infallible canon of Scripture as determined by the fallible church, as she was led by the Spirit. Dr. Lutzer concludes this chapter with a description of how the canon came to be.

Personal Response

Part of the argument against the veracity of the Bible is that it has gone through so many revisions and languages that it can hardly be trusted as reliable or true. Get a copy of the *New Living Translation* of the Bible and read through the article at the front entitled "Introduction to the *New Living Translation*." Find the answers to the following questions:

1. What is the intent of the translation team?

2. What is the purpose of the translation?

3. What texts did the scholars use in the translation of the text?

4. What is a dynamic-equivalence translation?

5. What does this mean for the reader of the *New Living Translation*?

6. How is this "dynamic-equivalence" formed?

7. Who are the scholars who translated and reviewed the material?

If you have time, compare these notes with those of other popular translations such as the NIV, ESV, and NKJV.

1. What do you find in common?

2. Are there dissimilarities? If so, what are they?

Take some time this week to sit with your Bible. If you have access to more than one translation, consider setting them side by side and comparing them as you read a passage. Compare the date of publication, the publisher, the words used, the language style, tone, punctuation, etc., to get a grasp of the differences in translations and the reasons for these differences.

A SUCCESSFUL
SEARCH FOR JESUS

Quiz

1. What is the name of the organization that meets to discuss and vote on the validity of the sayings of Jesus?

2. What percent of Jesus' sayings would this organization attribute to Jesus' actual sayings?

3. According to the Jesus Seminar, is Jesus more than a man?

4. In the book, *The Five Gospels*, what are the five Gospels?

5. Scholars believe that in order to find the true historical Jesus, those studying the Gospels should evaluate them as any other historical work. True or False?

6. What are the tests that John Warwick Montgomery suggests for testing the accuracy of the New Testament documents? For extra credit, give a brief statement of what each test means (pp. 111–115).

7. What is the approximate gap in years between the original and the copies of New Testament texts?

8. What is the approximate gap in years for copies of Plato's works?

9. Were any of the books of the New Testament written by eyewitnesses?

10. What doctrinal truth about Christ would have been outrageous for any practicing Jew to believe?

Chapter Summary

Dr. Lutzer opens this chapter with a short review of the Jesus Seminar, an organization that meets semiannually in California. During their meetings, members cast votes (colored beads) on whether they believe various Jesus events and teachings recorded in the Bible are historical. They have concluded that only about 18 percent of what is attributed to Jesus is actually true. And those statements and activities fit nicely into modern hot topics like feminism, ecology, and political correctness. These scholars, however, do not support the possibility of miracles and the supernatural. In fact, the founder of the Jesus Seminar stated that a person couldn't believe the New Testament version of Jesus, after having seen the cosmos through Galileo's telescope (p. 105).

Dr. Lutzer follows this introduction by emphasizing the responsibility readers and scholars have to respect the historicity of documents and to not pick and choose based on personal liking and comfort levels. To make decisions based on personal whim or comfort is to create history in the eyes of the beholder with little or no accountability to dozens or hundreds of other supporting records that validate the account. If there is no responsibility, the reader can "make sense" of the miracles and claims to lordship by saying Jesus was crazy, deluded, or fanatical, but surely not the Messiah. Dr. Lutzer states that the reader is faced with a clear choice: *Either accept Jesus as he is portrayed in the New Testament or confess ignorance about him.*

Next Dr. Lutzer develops the validity of the New Testament texts through an evaluation method that considers three aspects of the documents under consideration. The first is the *biographical test*, which asks the question, "If we do not have the original, by what means do we have the current copies, and is this tradition reliable?" The second test, the *internal test*, questions the claims of the writer of the work. The internal test determines whether the writer was an eyewitness, knew the author, was somewhat related to the work, or has no real connection to the work (a pseudepigrapha). The third test is the *external test*. This test compares the present material with other historical documents to see if other documents support the same facts, events, ideas, or people.

Dr. Lutzer addresses the eyewitness testimonies of the disciples and other followers as valid. He states with support that the disciples would not have raised these claims that Jesus was the Messiah, the Son of God, on their own. In other New Testament documents, letters to churches and individuals, we see eyewitnesses, Peter, James, and John advocating for Jesus, saying they saw these activities with their own eyes. They not only saw; they also heard and touched him following the resurrection. These followers can confirm the prophecies that Christ fulfilled. They confirm what we read in the New Testament. They are witnesses to the activities and claims of Christ.

Personal Response

This week, read the account of the Prodigal Son in Luke 15. This is the final parable in a series of parables about lost items: the lost sheep, the lost coin, and the lost son. If you have access to the *Life Application Bible*, review the study notes to understand what is going on in the text and why certain aspects of the story are significant.

Meditate on this passage. Spend time reading and rereading—placing yourself in the story and imagining the feelings of various characters: the father, the younger son, the older brother, a servant, a friend of the father, and so on. Then look back at the passage. Circle, underline, and memorize segments of Scripture that are poignant statements about the mercy and grace that flows from the Father.

As you read, answer these questions:

1. What did it mean that the younger son asked for his inheritance?

2. In verse 17, what does it mean when this son "came to his senses"?

3. Watch the older brother's response. What is his argument to his father?

4. With which brother do you most identify? Why? When?

5. When have you held resentment for what others have done to wrong you? Or against those who seem to have received more mercy than you?

6. Why do you think you responded that way?

7. What does the older brother's bitterness indicate?

8. In what way did the father show mercy to the younger brother?

9. Who does the father represent in this passage?

10. In what way(s) have you received mercy in lieu of punishment for your errors?

11. What truth(s) can you glean from this story about the Father?

12. How is this mercy possible for us today in the twenty-first century?

13. What is required of believers as we understand this passage?

DIVERGENT PATHS: THE CHURCH AND ITS COMPETITORS

Quiz

1. Some have said Jesus stole the identity and history of what pagan god?

2. Name one of two books Dr. Lutzer mentions where a reader can find prophecy about Jesus.

3. Do Gnostics believe in the necessity of the death and resurrection of Jesus?

4. Gnostics use the word *logos* as a term that means what?

5. In what Gnostic book is the resurrection of Christ referred to as a vision, dream, or trance?

6. According to Gnosticism, the person's spiritual problem is _____, not _____.

7. The doctrine that all men and women are born into a state of sin is called what?

8. True or False: Jesus could have saved people without being either human or divine.

9. True or False: Muslims believe that Jesus was God incarnate.

Chapter Summary

In the first half of the chapter, Dr. Lutzer lays out what Christianity is not. In the first few paragraphs, he alludes to scholars who have reduced Christianity to a list of stolen mythological facts from the legend of Mithras, popular in ancient Rome. Mithras is understood to be a god of the ancient Persians and was known as the "son of God, the Light of the world." Supposedly, he was born on December 25, died, was buried in a rock tomb, and rose from the dead three days later. However, as Dr. Lutzer states, Jesus was prophesied in the Old Testament seven centuries before Christ; those prophecies were fulfilled in the life and work of Christ. Gnosticism is a perversion and a tangent from the true gospel of Christ. It appeals to people today, to their desire to connect with the metaphysical world. A Gnostic teaching will allow the adherent to essentially choose his or her own path, selecting what he or she likes and dislikes.

In order to deal with people's need for salvation, the Jesus captured in the Gospel narrative must be real; he must be true. The acts of healing, the forgiving of sins, the raising of dead people, the teachings, and the fulfilling of prophecy must be real, not imaginary. To name them as mirages is to remove the ability of Jesus to be Savior, who mediates for believers at the right hand of God the Father. In removing Christ's divinity and making his death a ruse, Gnostics believe that we encounter God in ourselves, in our divine inner spark of enlightenment, our "gnosis." Flying in the face of Scripture that tells of our sinful state, Gnosticism says we are not sinful, just ignorant.

Gnosticism is not another viable version of Christianity. In addition, we cannot mix and match what we like best from the world's religions, or claim they are all equal options.

How is Christianity different than what we see in other religions? First, we find the doctrine of sin—the truth that all people, in all times and all places, are affected by original sin. Everyone is born with a sin nature that causes actual sins, which we commit and which are committed against us. Second, everyone is held to a perfect law from a perfect God. In order to be in the presence of God, we must be perfect. Third, Jesus comes on the scene as the God-man, fully God and fully human, able to bridge the divide and meet the demands of the penalty of sin: death. The Incarnate Word, the Savior, Jesus is the connection between God and people, and he is the only possible connection. We cannot earn salvation; we cannot achieve it on our own, as Gnosticism and other religions profess.

We cannot change God into our own liking; we cannot make him as we wish; we cannot approach him through any means other than faith in the saving work of Jesus Christ. This is the Good News—the faith we profess in Jesus Christ. To put our hope in our own works and efforts to be enlightened is bad news for sure.

Personal Response

In the space below, write out, or if you have a recorder, tape yourself sharing the gospel, the story of sinful men and women redeemed and forgiven through the work of Jesus Christ on the cross. Afterward, listen to yourself and write down the main points.

1. What did you forget to mention?

Go back to Scripture and find passages that communicate the gospel and a sinner's need for salvation. What in the story of the gospel really resonates with you? Why?

1. Your sin?

2. God's love?

3. God's grace?

4. Christ's suffering?

Pray for an opportunity this week to share this message with someone you know: a family member, friend, or colleague.